COOKING *with* MISS QUAD

COOKING *with* MISS QUAD

LIVE, LAUGH, LOVE, *and* EAT

Quad Webb

Foreword by Pat Neely

THE COUNTRYMAN PRESS

A division of W. W. Norton & Company

Independent Publishers Since 1923

For information about permission to reproduce selections from this book, write to
Permissions, The Countryman Press, 500 Fifth Avenue, New York, NY 10110

For information about special discounts for bulk purchases, please contact
W. W. Norton Special Sales at specialsales@wwnorton.com or 800-233-4830

Manufacturing by LSC Communications, Willard
Book design by LeAnna Weller Smith
Production manager: Devon Zahn

The Countryman Press
www.countrymanpress.com

A division of W. W. Norton & Company, Inc.
500 Fifth Avenue, New York, NY 10110
www.wwnorton.com

978-1-68268-380-4

10 9 8 7 6 5 4 3 2 1

This book is dedicated to my father, the first man to love me.

Daddy, you are my hero, my partner, my friend, and one of my biggest supporters.
You taught me how to love unconditionally, instilling in me self-worth and confidence.
You taught me about life and broadening my horizons.

Thank you for the life lessons, for your patience,
and for helping me to become a woman who moves without fear.
I appreciate you teaching me to always believe in myself and take risks.

In short, I want to thank you for the jewels you've placed in my crown.

I love you!

Contents

Foreword

BY PAT NEELY

Hey, ya'll, let me tell you a little something about Miss Quad. Millions of you see her vibrant personality every day as cohost of the hit talk show, *Sister Circle*, and millions more love watching her sweet and sassy side each week on Bravo's hit reality show, *Married to Medicine*. Like you, I was a fan before I ever met her, and just as I thought, she is fantastic and this lady can cook!

My first meeting with Miss Quad was on the set of *Sister Circle*. As cameras rolled, I swiftly learned the Memphis beauty had serious skills in the kitchen just by the way we bonded over ingredients and flavors. The moments that we cooked together, we created a connection over our love for food.

See, Miss Quad is a true Memphis girl who knows how to give you that down-home Southern meal with a modern-day flair, which she accomplishes by incorporating the rhythm of the city with the blues of the people, giving you a meal that is filled with soul. Although she has the taste of Memphis at her fingertips, she has a palate that reaches far and wide.

I am delighted to see that Miss Quad is opening up her kitchen and sharing her recipes with you. With every dish, you will be privy to a personal side of the lady that I now call my friend. From her spicy twist on mouthwatering shrimp to her signature cocktails, such as Blueberry Bourbon Lemonade, Miss Quad ain't playing around and you can taste the love with every bite.

You can't go wrong with any of these delicious recipes. Now, go ahead, turn the page and enjoy these brilliant dishes.

Introduction

When I was a young doll, the kitchen was where we congregated as a family. My mom and I shared special bonding time there, talking and laughing—and then, before I knew it, a meal had been prepared. My mom always presented cooking as fun and exciting, which made me eager to pitch in. For me, cooking is neither a chore nor a daunting task that looms over my head throughout the day. Cooking is my refuge. In the kitchen, I am in my comfort zone and for the longest time I thought everyone shared the same cosmic experience I have while cooking, until I saw the panic that possessed my friends when confronted with the thought of being in the kitchen.

This inspired the #CookingwithQuad tutorials, where I invite viewers into my kitchen so that they can truly see how gratifying and rewarding cooking should be, especially when you are able to enjoy your creation and share it with the ones you love. As I received a tremendous amount of support and gratitude from the tutorials, I became very interested in the source of that trepidation, and I've discovered it boils down to kitchen intimidation. People put too much pressure on themselves. The kitchen is not a fire-breathing dragon that cannot be tamed, you just need a guide to get you past your fear and your butterflies. Just like you have to let your guard down to truly experience love, you have to become vulnerable in the kitchen.

Now I love technology just as much as the next person. Let's be real, that's how this book idea came to life, but technology has become a major distraction and made it harder to connect with family and loved

ones. It's no wonder why, a majority of the time, people are on their phones more than they are communicating with the one right in front of them.

I, like so many others, wear many hats. As a talk show host, BCBG brand contributor, and television personality, not to mention founder and CEO of Picture Perfect Pup, I find that the hours of the day seem to just fly by! In a world where schedules are full and time is scarce, we have moved beyond reservations and carryout, and progressed to apps such as GrubHub and UberEats for our food. In my opinion, we need to get back to the basics of cooking and take it up a notch by setting the atmosphere with inviting lighting, music, amazing cocktails, and place settings. Turn your home into your own cozy bistro.

I learned long ago that it is important to keep recipes fun and fresh while cooking. The food you consume can have a direct impact on your life, affecting your hormones, brain chemistry, energy, and stress levels. The kitchen allows you to be creative, spontaneous, and daring. It's a safe place to take risks, but be sure that the dish tastes good before you serve it to your guests!

Cooking is all about trusting yourself so that you are comfortable and confident enough to be free to create. Cooking requires you to use all of your senses as you prepare meals. You have to touch, taste, smell, see, and hear what's going on in the kitchen.

I wrote this book to remove the assumption that it takes hours slaving over a hot stove to prepare a great meal. This book is filled with recipes that will serve as your guide to creating fun and flavorful dishes. I will teach you how to avoid common faux pas and provide you with tips on how to be the "it-girl or -guy" who commands the kitchen. I will share with you the essential utensils and must-have foods for your pantry. I'll get you

whipped into shape and have you ready to throw down at your next dinner party.

When I tell you that I have seen it all, I mean it. I have friends who are successful in so many areas but cannot find their way around the kitchen. They constantly call me to whip up a meal for them to impress their family, friends, or someone they are dating, after they've promised to prepare a delectable dining experience.

I have been on the phone with a friend, who cannot boil water, listening to her describe a savory meal that she has planned for her dinner date. A meal that sounds so good that I want to try it, but little did I know that I would be the one preparing it. I cannot even recall how many fake-and-bake, drive-by, and meal drop-offs that I have made throughout the years. It's to the point where the requests have become "just meet me at the corner," and I find myself giving them their catch-a-man-meal at the local corner store, leaving them with the only instructions I pray that they can remember: warm it up and don't let it sit too long!

Cooking with Miss Quad will provide the blueprint to end these cooking woes. I am equipping you with the essentials, mixed with a dash of love to make you confident and comfortable in the kitchen. I believe the ability to cook is in everyone, you just have to be determined and committed. If you follow these instructions and practice, you will begin to look at cooking like a romantic dance with pots and pans!

Just like my mom would always say, "The most important lesson in the kitchen is keeping the pace and the timing." Now, as a grown woman, that sounds like the rhythm of love to me! Cooking is a stress reliever, it's an expression of love, and I have made it my business to inspire others to become comfortable in the kitchen. Just look at me as your personal guide to becoming your own private chef. You can thank me later!

SETTING THE MOOD

Making sure you have the proper **utensils** is a fundamental aspect of preparing a meal, but it will take a little more than cookware to properly set the mood. So, let's explore methods to create the perfect canvas for a romantic dinner or an amazing dinner party for guests. Ambiance doesn't just happen. There are many factors to take into consideration, such as the environment, music, lighting, aroma, theme, and, believe or not, even the temperature.

We will start with the **environment**. The space must be clean, comfortable, and a desirable place to retreat. It should provide peace and tranquility that will allow your guests to be free from apprehension and eliminate any stresses of the daily hustle and bustle.

The next component is **temperature**, which is often overlooked. You don't want to arrange the perfect evening only to have it ruined because you didn't consider the proper temperature of the room. The climate shouldn't make you feel like you're living in an igloo, nor should it feel like you have died and gone to hell. Finding a comfortable temperature is a must, and your guests will appreciate it too!

Music is another element that appeals to the senses—it acts as the soundtrack to your wonderful evening. However, you can't play just any music, so for now put away the 2 Live Crew's Uncle Luke and your trap music. Soft, slow, and smooth music is always good to have playing in the background. Some of my favorites include Jodeci, Her, Rihanna, Beyoncé, Usher, Sade, Jhené Aiko, and Keith Sweat. If you aren't familiar with these artists, stick to something suave, such as George Benson, Frankie Beverly and Maze, or Anita Baker, and you can never go wrong with jazz.

Lighting is a key component to setting the perfect mood. Think back to your most treasured romantic vacations: were you on the beach overlooking the water as you watched the sunset and sipped a glass of wine? Or, were you walking hand in hand with your significant other at sunrise? Think of the feeling that you had in that very moment. Enchanting, right? Which means you already know how much lighting can make or break the mood. The proper use of lighting can allow you to completely change the makeup of the room. Stick with warm colors and avoid white blueish lights; you don't want it to be too bright (keep in mind that this is not a police interrogation).

This brings us to the most important element and really one of the reasons that I am writing this book: **aroma**. Fresh flowers and scented candles are great for setting the mood, but nothing compares to the delicious aromas that fill a room when you are preparing blackened seared scallops with sautéed green beans, or lamb chops with roasted potatoes and asparagus, or Cornish hens with sun-dried tomatoes. Nothing will heighten the senses of your guests or your date more than the intoxicating aroma from the homecooked meal you have prepared. Aromas can make you feel alive, alert, excited, and take you to a place of pleasure, joy, and happiness, whether it triggers a memory of spending time with family or visions of a romantic relationship. When determining the atmosphere, keep in mind that when people smell something good, they want to indulge and experience the taste. Aromas seal the deal for a lively evening!

When creating the theme of the evening, keep in mind that there is no one ideal tone to strike. The theme should be determined based on your understanding of your guests and the purpose of your soiree. It should be spontaneous, interesting, and new every time. For example, one night may be based around fun dancing while another is for playing board games while drinking wine. If it's a romantic moment, you may decide to draw a bubble bath sprinkled with rose petals. Moreover, the best theme can be no theme.

Presentation is very important, right down to the color of the plate you use. You want to be sure that you are simultaneously creating contrast and harmony in order to make the dish appealing to the eye. A white plate acts as a canvas for the artistry and the creativity of plating the food. When food is plated properly, it stimulates your senses and heightens your appetite. To create that irresistible look, be sure to play with bright and contrasting colors and take advantage of the different textures. The goal is to use as much color as possible; you may not be able to present all the colors in a bag of Skittles at every meal, but challenge yourself to use as many as you can.

I can't live a boring life, so why would I live with boring food? Enter **texture**! Different textures are pleasing because they influence creativity while cooking.

The way a food feels when you touch or eat it excites and delights the taste buds! Include flaky, crunchy, creamy, smooth, crumbly, soft, and gooey foods.

Whatever ambiance you decide to pursue, just remember to enjoy the moment and the new memories that you are creating with your family, friends, or lover. Don't become so consumed with checking everything off of the list that you miss the moment.

QUAD'S PANTRY

A list of must-have food and seasoning essentials for every kitchen.

COOKING TOOLS

Avocado slicer

Baking sheet

Blender

Boiling pot

Can opener

Cast-iron frying pan

Cheese grater

Cutting board

Dutch oven

Indoor grill

Knife

Ladle

Large frying pan

Measuring cups

Measuring spoons

Mixing bowl

Perforated spoon

Rice steamer

Saucepan

Serving spoon

Slow cooker

Spatula

Strainer

Tongs

Wine opener

ESSENTIAL INGREDIENTS

All-purpose flour

Bell peppers (red, orange, and yellow)

Black pepper

Browning seasoning

Butter

Cajun spice mix

Capers

Cayenne pepper

Celery

Chicken broth

Cornmeal

Creole spice mix

Cumin

Eggs

Garlic

Garlic powder

Jasmine Rice

Ketchup

Kosher salt

Lemon juice

Mayonnaise

Milk

Mustard

Scallions

Soy sauce

Old Bay Seasoning

Olive oil

Olives

Onion powder

Onions

Panko bread crumbs

Paprika

Pink Himalayan salt

Potatoes

Red pepper flakes

Sugar

Vegetable oil

Worcestershire sauce

White wine

Yellow rice

FANCY *and* FREE, BREAKFAST IS *on* ME

Big breakfasts were for the weekends in my family. That was when we all sat down at the table to share details of our week. I've included my favorites here, which can also be served as brunch, for you to enjoy with your family and friends.

Spicy Sage Sausage Flatbread Topped with Fried Eggs   25

Potato, Ham, and Cheese Frittata   26

Bacon Cheddar Biscuits with Country Gravy   28

Creamy Yellowstone Grits with Scallion Butter Sauce   31

Savory Cornmeal Pancakes with Chive Cream Cheese   32

Mini Crab Cakes with Old Bay Aioli   35

Spicy Sage Sausage Flatbread Topped *with* Fried Eggs

MAKES 4 FLATBREADS

Breakfast staples can become a little boring, so I like to find different ways to spice them up! This recipe is one of my favorites because it is super simple to make and will definitely impress your brunch guests. The fried egg is the pièce de résistance because it not only adds protein but the egg on top looks magnificent! Serve these with my favorite Prosecco Spritzers (page 215), garnished with fresh and festive pomegranate seeds.

FLATBREAD

2 large prepared flatbreads
    (or pizza rounds)

1 pound ground spicy pork sausage

¾ cup sliced shiitake mushrooms

½ teaspoon dried sage

½ teaspoon freshly ground black
    pepper

1 red chile pepper, thinly sliced

2 Roma tomatoes, diced

1 cup shredded Colby Jack

Fresh sage leaves (optional)

Chopped chives, for garnish

FRIED EGGS

1½ teaspoons unsalted butter

4 large eggs

Pink Himalayan salt

Prepare the flatbreads: Preheat a grill to medium heat or warm a frying pan on the stove. Cut each flatbread in half and toast both sides on grill or pan. Place breads on a parchment-lined baking sheet.

Heat a skillet over high heat and sauté the pork sausage and shiitake mushrooms until the sausage has an internal temperature of 160°F. Season with the sage and black pepper. Remove from the heat and set aside.

Sprinkle the flatbreads evenly with the red chile pepper and tomatoes. Top with the pork sausage mixture, cheese, and sage leaves, if using.

Place under the broiler and broil for 4 minutes, or until golden brown and the toppings are crispy and juicy. Set aside.

Prepare the fried eggs: Lightly spray a skillet with nonstick cooking spray, add the butter and melt over medium heat.

Crack each egg directly into pan and allow the membrane to fry lightly. Turn heat to low and cook until yolk is set, for sunny-side up. If you prefer, once a crust begins to form, flip the egg in its entirety, creating a pouch to protect yolk. Let fry for 1 to 2 minutes.

Remove the eggs from skillet, season with salt, and place directly on the flatbread. Garnish with chopped chives. Serve immediately.

Potato, Ham, *and* Cheese Frittata

SERVES 4

I didn't eat a frittata until I was an adult, but now I'm making up for lost time. A frittata is basically an omelet with potatoes, an elegant take on ham and eggs, or a quiche without a crust. It's a lot easier to make than quiche, and tastes good hot or cold. To keep my frittata full of flavor, I use smoked Gouda and country ham. The red bliss potatoes provide a substantial bite that will keep you going for hours.

7 large eggs

⅓ cup whole milk

½ teaspoon kosher salt

¼ teaspoon freshly ground
    white pepper

¼ cup olive oil

4 red bliss potatoes, thinly sliced

1 sweet yellow onion, thinly sliced

¼ cup chopped scallions

1 cup shredded baby spinach

1 cup diced salted country ham

½ cup shredded smoked Gouda

1 ripe tomato, sliced (optional)

Preheat the oven to 375°F.

Stir together the eggs, milk, salt, and pepper in a medium bowl.

Heat the oil until shimmering in a large cast-iron skillet over medium heat. Add the potatoes and onion and sauté until tender, 5 minutes. Then add the scallions and spinach and sauté for another 5 minutes.

Pour the egg mixture into the skillet. Let the eggs rest undisturbed for about 20 seconds, then begin to lift the eggs in circular motion. After about a minute, when the mixture begins to set, distribute the ham and cheese evenly on top of the eggs. Lay tomato slices on top, if using.

Remove from the heat and transfer the pan to the oven. Bake for about 8 minutes, or until raised and golden brown.

Tip: I like to serve individual frittatas in mini cast-iron skillets. Just divide the egg mixture, once it begins to set, into the smaller pans. Bake for about 5 minutes or until set.

Bacon Cheddar Biscuits *with* Country Gravy

MAKES ABOUT 12 BISCUITS

If you love those Cheddar biscuits at the very well-known seafood restaurant chain, then you're gonna love my bacon Cheddar biscuits. Remixed with a Southern twist, they are very simple to make and can be served at any time of the day. Topped with country gravy, they make a meal all on their own! Trust me, these biscuits are a five-star recipe.

BACON CHEDDAR BISCUITS

2 cups all-purpose flour, plus more for dusting

2 teaspoons baking powder

¾ teaspoon baking soda

½ teaspoon kosher salt

2 teaspoons granulated sugar

5 tablespoons cold unsalted butter, diced

4 slices cooked bacon, chopped, plus additional for serving

½ cup shredded Cheddar

¾ cup buttermilk

COUNTRY GRAVY

2 tablespoons European-style butter

½ sweet yellow onion, finely chopped

½ pound pork sausage

2½ tablespoons all-purpose flour

⅛ ground kosher salt

¼ teaspoon freshly ground black pepper

2 cups whole milk

Preheat the oven to 425°F. Lightly spray a large baking sheet with nonstick cooking spray.

Stir together the flour, baking powder, baking soda, salt, and sugar in a large bowl. Cut in the butter until the mixture has a sandy consistency.

Stir in the bacon and Cheddar. Pour in the buttermilk and stir until the dough comes together. Form into a ball.

On a floured countertop, knead the ball of dough about ten times, then pat it out into in a ½-inch square.

Use a 2- or 3-inch round biscuit cutter to cut out disks and place on the prepared baking sheet. Bake the biscuits for 15 to 17 minutes, until golden brown.

Meanwhile, prepare the gravy: Melt the butter in a medium skillet over medium heat. Add the onion and cook until completely caramelized, about 10 minutes. Add the sausage, breaking it up into small pieces with a wooden spoon. Cook, stirring occasionally, until no longer pink, 5 to 7 minutes.

Stir together the flour, salt, and pepper in a small bowl. Add to the sausage mixture and toss gently to coat. Cook over medium-high heat until golden brown.

Stir in the milk and bring to a boil. Stirring constantly, lower the heat to low and cook until the gravy reaches your desired thickness. Taste and season with more salt and black pepper, if needed.

Serve the biscuits with gravy and additional bacon, if desired.

Creamy Yellowstone Grits
with Scallion Butter Sauce

SERVES 4 TO 6

Grits are a tasty comfort food that offer a break from the usual morning routine. I like this recipe because it's not only creamy, but also buttery and brimming with flavor, thanks to the fresh scallions. I'm a savory gal and I like the peppery sharp crunch of scallions. This dish is great on its own, but adding shrimp or pairing with steak and eggs creates a meal that will leave you completely satisfied.

CREAMY YELLOWSTONE GRITS

1 cup heavy cream

⅔ cup water

2 tablespoons unsalted butter

½ teaspoon kosher salt

½ teaspoon freshly ground black pepper

1 cup chicken stock

1 cup Yellowstone grits

SCALLION BUTTER SAUCE

8 tablespoons (1 stick) European-style butter, at room temperature

2 scallions, trimmed and chopped

Pink Himalayan salt, to taste

Freshly ground black pepper, to taste

Prepare the grits: Combine the cream and water in a large saucepan and bring to a rolling boil. Add the butter and the salt and pepper. Bring back to a boil and add the chicken stock.

Lower the heat to medium and slowly whisk in the grits, stirring constantly to prevent lumping. Reduce the heat to low and allow the grits to cook slowly for 16 to 20 minutes. They should have the consistency of smooth and creamy butter. Taste and add additional salt and pepper, if needed.

While grits are cooking, prepare the sauce: Melt the butter in a small saucepan over low heat. Stir in the scallions. Season with the salt and pepper to taste and serve atop the grits.

Note: If you don't have time to make the scallion butter sauce, just top your grits wil a pat of butter. Easy!

Savory Cornmeal Pancakes
with Chive Cream Cheese

SERVES 4

When you think of pancakes, you probably picture fluffy, sweet, round cakes smothered in butter and syrup, but you know me, I love to switch things up! I changed up the entire concept of pancakes by making them full-bodied and savory. I add a cream cheese and chive topping for a unique twist. If you're in the mood, serve with crisp bacon or spicy sausage. Now that's some good eating!

PANCAKES

1 cup yellow cornmeal

1 cup all-purpose flour

1½ teaspoons baking powder

1 teaspoon kosher salt

2 large eggs

Vegetable oil

1 cup whole milk

CHIVE CREAM CHEESE

4 tablespoons (½ stick) unsalted butter

¼ cup chopped chives

2 fresh garlic cloves, minced

3 tablespoons dry white wine

3 tablespoons vegetable stock

1 (8-ounce) package cream cheese, diced

½ teaspoon kosher salt

Prepare the pancakes: Stir together the cornmeal, flour, baking powder, and salt in a large bowl.

Stir together the eggs, 3 tablespoons of the oil, and the milk in a small bowl.

Add the wet ingredients to the dry and combine well into a creamy batter. Set aside.

Prepare the chive cream cheese: Melt the butter in a small saucepan over medium heat and add the chives and garlic. Simmer for 2 minutes.

Add the wine and stock. Simmer for about 5 minutes.

Drop the diced cream cheese into the simmering mixture and whisk gently. Continue to whisk over low heat until all the cream cheese is incorporated. Season with salt. Remove from the heat until ready to serve.

When you're ready to eat, and the cream cheese has been prepared, heat 1 to 2 inches oil in a stock pot or Dutch oven over medium heat.

When oil is hot enough to cook a drop of batter, drop pancakes into oil with a large spoon. (You will need to cook them in batches.) Flip after about 3 minutes, then cook until the pancakes are golden brown. Transfer to a plate and cook the remaining batter.

Rewarm the cream cheese if necessary. Serve pancakes topped with the cream cheese.

Note: You can also simply top pancakes with ready-made chive cream cheese or plain cream cheese with minced chives.

Mini Crab Cakes *with* Old Bay Aioli

MAKES 12 PATTIES

I'm a seafood lover, and I always opt to serve these mini crab cakes above all else to make a classy statement. I like to pair these with a savory aioli for a welcome bit of sass. Don't let the name scare you—it's simple. I start with prepared mayo and make it mine with Old Bay Seasoning.

OLD BAY AIOLI

½ cup mayonnaise

2 teaspoons Dijon mustard

½ teaspoon cider vinegar

1 teaspoon Old Bay Seasoning

CRAB CAKES

1 pound jumbo lump crabmeat

½ cup mayonnaise

1 tablespoon Dijon mustard

1 tablespoon Worcestershire sauce

2 tablespoons minced fresh chives

2 teaspoons Old Bay Seasoning

½ teaspoon kosher salt

½ teaspoon freshly ground black pepper

Juice of 1 lemon

1 cup Italian bread crumbs

Prepare the aioli: Combine all the aioli ingredients in a small bowl, cover with plastic wrap, and refrigerate until ready to serve.

Prepare the crab cakes: Preheat the oven to 425°F. Evenly coat a rimmed cookie sheet with the cooking spray.

Combine all the crab cake ingredients, except the bread crumbs, in a bowl. Divide the mixture equally into 1-inch patties, making 12 mini patties.

Pour the bread crumbs into a shallow bowl or pie pan. Lightly and evenly coat the crab cake patties on both sides with the bread crumbs.

Place the patties on the prepared cookie sheet. Bake until the tops begin to brown, 15 to 20 minutes.

Serve with the aioli.

TEASERS BUT *Surely* PLEASERS

Appetizers set the tone for the evening. They will signal to your guests whether or not you have what it takes to move on to a main course. Trust me, these nibblers build intrigue for whatever comes next. Serve them on their own, too, as hearty snacks, perfect for cocktail time or halftime.

Lemon Pepper Hot Wings

MAKES 24 WINGS

Let's elevate the hot wing with a glass of good Champagne. Why not? My recipe is spicy as expected, but with a hint of tart from the lemon pepper. I bake the wings twice to up the crunch factor; be careful when you're coating them with sauce right from the oven, as they're piping hot and it can get messy.

24 chicken wings, separated at joint, tips discarded (about 2 pounds)

RUB

3 tablespoons lemon pepper, plus more for sprinkling

1 teaspoon garlic powder

½ teaspoon cayenne pepper

SAUCE

8 tablespoons (1 stick) unsalted butter

1 (12-ounce) bottle hot sauce

2 tablespoons Worcestershire sauce

Preheat the oven to 450°F. Line a baking sheet with aluminum foil and place a wire rack on top. Spray the rack with oil.

Pat the wings dry with paper towels to remove as much moisture as possible.

Prepare the rub: Stir together the lemon pepper, garlic powder, and cayenne in a large bowl. A few wings at a time, add the wings to the bowl and mix to evenly coat.

Place the wings on the wire rack in a single layer and spray with oil. Roast in the oven for 30 minutes, turning once halfway through cooking.

Meanwhile, prepare the sauce: Melt the butter in a small saucepan. Remove from the heat and stir in the hot sauce and Worcestershire until combined.

Remove the wings from the oven and, using tongs, carefully transfer them to a large bowl. Pour the sauce over the wings, in batches if necessary, and toss to coat.

Turn on the broiler and spray the wire rack again. Place the sauced wings on the rack in a single layer. Sprinkle the wings with lemon pepper and spray with oil. Broil the wings on HIGH until crispy and slightly charred, 2 to 3 minutes. Remove from oven and sprinkle with a little more lemon pepper for zest.

New Orleans–Style BBQ Shrimp

SERVES 4 TO 6

Being in New Orleans is nothing but a good ole time, and there is nothing like food inspired by the Big Easy to remind you of pure bliss. I prefer to make these plump and spicy jumbo shrimp with the shell on, so that you can get down and dirty while savoring the hot sauce on each fingertip. This is an excellent appetizer solo or paired with grits for a real Mardi Gras in your mouth.

¼ cup Creole seasoning

½ teaspoon cayenne pepper (optional)

1 teaspoon dried thyme

1 teaspoon kosher salt

1 teaspoon freshly ground black pepper

2 pounds extra-large shrimp, shells on

Olive oil, as needed

2 large shallots, minced

4 garlic cloves, minced

3 tablespoons Worcestershire sauce

¼ cup dry white wine

2 tablespoons fresh lemon juice

Hot sauce, to taste

Stir together the Creole seasoning, cayenne (if using), thyme, salt, and pepper in a large bowl. Add the shrimp, coat evenly, and set aside.

Heat the oil in a large skillet over medium-high heat, using enough oil to coat the pan. Sauté the shallots and garlic until the shallots are soft, 3 minutes.

Stir in the Worcestershire and white wine. Add the shrimp and sauté just until they turn pink and opaque. Add the lemon juice and a few dashes of hot sauce to taste.

Serve immediately.

Ahi Tuna Ceviche

SERVES 2 TO 4

This flavorful dish has a good texture that is titillating to the taste buds. The aromatic scent of the onions and the freshness of the cilantro add excitement without overpowering the fresh taste of the tuna. I like to serve this appetizer in a martini glass to add a little panache to an easy-to-make hors d'oeuvre.

2 Roma tomatoes, diced

2 tablespoons thinly chopped scallion

2 tablespoons chopped fresh cilantro

1 jalapeño pepper, seeded and minced

1 teaspoon minced fresh ginger

2 tablespoons soy sauce

1 teaspoon Asian fish sauce

Kosher salt and freshly ground black pepper

½ pound sushi-grade ahi tuna, cubed

¼ cup fresh lime juice

¼ teaspoon black sesame seeds

Combine the tomatoes, scallion, cilantro, jalapeño, ginger, soy sauce, and fish sauce in a bowl large enough to hold the tuna. Taste the mixture and add salt and black pepper to taste, if needed.

Add the tuna to the bowl and mix until thoroughly coated. Add the lime juice and black sesame seeds. Serve immediately.

Tip: If cooked tuna is preferred, after adding the lime juice to the mixture, cover and refrigerate for 1 to 3 hours. The acid from the lime will "cook" the tuna, which will turn an opaque grayish color.

Don't blow your top by applying unnecessary pressure.

"S o often in life we get caught up in how we think things should be, feel, and look that we forget to be fully present or allow ourselves to live in the now and enjoy the moment.

A prime example: My girl Michelle always placed an overwhelming amount of pressure on herself when it came to cooking. She was so used to being really good at so many things that she shied away from cooking because she wasn't comfortable. It was not that she couldn't follow directions, she just didn't trust herself in the kitchen and didn't like the feeling of not being in control. Her intimidation would grow, and she would talk herself out of being open to learning her way around the kitchen. I recently ran across a quote that suits this situation perfectly, and it happens to come from someone who I admire very much as an actor and human being: Will Smith. Will brilliantly stated, "The best things in life are on the other side of terror."

Michelle and I had several conversations surrounding her intimidation of cooking and I was finally able to convince her to let me teach her to cook. I quickly realized that before I could begin to teach her the basics, we had to change her mindset. She had to understand that it is okay to make mistakes and that, as long as she tried, she would surely conquer her fear of cooking.

Memphis BBQ Pork Nachos

SERVES 6 TO 8

If your family members are sports fanatics, then I have the perfect cheesy, meaty, crunchy snack to make them scream "touchdown!" You'll score big points with slow-cooked pulled pork that is extremely tender and deliciously savory in my signature BBQ sauce. Add a few jalapeños for heat and you'll be the real MVP.

1 (16-ounce) bag tortilla chips

1 pound Memphis BBQ Pulled Pork (see page 196)

1 cup shredded sharp Cheddar

1 cup shredded pepper Jack

1 large red onion, diced

2 to 3 jalapeños, sliced into rings, or 1 (6-ounce) jar pickled jalapeño peppers

Preheat the oven to 450°F. Line a baking sheet with aluminum foil.

Prepare the nachos: Spread the tortilla chips evenly on the prepared baking sheet. Top the chips with the pulled pork in a single layer. Cover with the Cheddar and pepper Jack. Bake until the cheese melts completely, 10 minutes.

Garnish with the red onion and jalapeños and serve immediately.

Tip: This is an easy recipe to double...or triple!

Stuffed Mushrooms
with Creamed Spinach *and* Bacon

MAKES 24 MUSHROOMS

I find that whenever you add bacon, you can never go wrong. These bite-size apps are hard to resist, with smoky bacon complementing the tangy taste of the cream cheese and Monterey Jack. They taste great with a pinot noir.

STUFFING MIXTURE

2 teaspoons olive oil, plus
　　more for brushing

1 small shallot, minced

4 garlic cloves, minced

1 cup loosely-packed spinach, shredded

6 slices thick-cut bacon, cooked and
　　crumbled

1 (8-ounce) package cream cheese,
　　softened

¼ cup shredded Monterey Jack, plus
　　more for sprinkling

1 teaspoon freshly ground black pepper

1 teaspoon kosher salt

1 teaspoon onion powder

1 teaspoon chili powder

MUSHROOMS

24 Baby Bella mushrooms, cleaned,
　　stems and gills removed

¼ cup bread crumbs

Preheat the oven to 350°F. Line a baking sheet with parchment paper.

Prepare the stuffing: Heat the oil in a large skillet. Sauté the shallot and garlic for 2 to 3 minutes. Add the spinach and sauté for an additional minute. Remove the skillet from the heat.

Stir together the bacon, cream cheese, Monterey Jack, pepper, salt, onion powder, and chili powder in a bowl until fully combined.

Prepare the mushrooms: Brush the mushrooms with oil to coat evenly. Use a teaspoon to fill each mushroom with the stuffing mixture. Place the mushrooms, stuffing side up, on the prepared baking sheet. Sprinkle with additional Monterey Jack and the bread crumbs. Bake for 20 minutes. Serve hot or at room temperature.

Tip: For no-fuss bacon, cook it on a sheet pan in the oven. Place a wire rack on top of a parchment-lined baking sheet and arrange the bacon in a single layer on the rack. Bake for 12 to 15 minutes at 425°F, until it is crispy. Remove from the oven and set aside to cool.

Chorizo Queso Dip

SERVES 4 TO 6

Mexican food has a way of being very comforting and filling. This is one of those dips that I love to share with a friend over cocktails and a good kee-kee. What makes this dish so delish is how the combination of the oils and spices from the sausage mix with the sharp cheese. I like to add a little jalapeño pepper for heat, and cilantro gives it a fresh and healthy taste and pop of color. Pair with tortilla chips or baked pita bread and a glass of white wine to have a great time.

1 cup shredded sharp Cheddar

1 cup shredded Monterey Jack or Oaxaca

1 (8-ounce) package cream cheese, softened

2 tablespoons olive oil

1 large yellow onion, diced

3 garlic cloves, minced

1 pound chorizo sausage, casings removed

1 large jalapeño pepper, sliced fresh or pickled

¼ cup fresh cilantro (optional)

Tortilla chips, for serving

Preheat the oven to 375°F.

Spray a small casserole dish or oven-safe pan with nonstick cooking spray. In a small bowl, combine the Cheddar, Monterey Jack, and cream cheese. Scrape into dish and bake for 20 minutes.

Heat the oil in a large skillet over medium-high heat, then sauté the onion and garlic until the onion becomes translucent, 3 to 5 minutes. Add the chorizo to the pan and break it up with your spatula while sautéing until the sausage has browned, 5 to 7 minutes.

Using a slotted spoon, transfer the chorizo mixture to a paper towel to drain.

When ready, remove cheese from oven and top with the chorizo mixture, jalapeño, and cilantro, if using. Serve immediately with tortilla chips.

Cajun Deviled Eggs

MAKES 16 EGGS

These eggs are not your typical deviled eggs. They are made extra smooth in the food processor with cream cheese and mayonnaise. To make them feisty, I add a little hot sauce, and for color and texture, I add minced chives. Want to up your game and make them fancy for a dinner party? Add a cooked shrimp in the middle, garnish with parsley, and watch these bites disappear.

8 large hard-boiled eggs

2 tablespoons cream cheese

3 tablespoons mayonnaise

1 tablespoon Dijon mustard

2 teaspoons hot sauce

1 teaspoon onion powder

1 teaspoon chili powder

1 teaspoon freshly ground black pepper

¼ teaspoon ground cumin

Kosher salt

Hot sauce (optional)

Cayenne pepper, for garnish (optional)

Minced chives, for garnish (optional)

Cut the eggs in half lengthwise and scoop the yolks into a food processor. Add the cream cheese, mayonnaise, Dijon, hot sauce, onion powder, chili powder, black pepper, and cumin and process until the mixture becomes smooth. Taste and add salt as needed.

Fill a piping bag with the yolk mixture. Pipe each egg white half with the yolk mixture.

Top with hot sauce, if using, or a sprinkle of cayenne and minced chives, if desired.

Note: If you don't have a piping bag, you can snip off the corner of a sandwich bag, or use a spoon. They will taste just as delicious.

Smoky Oven-Baked Potato Chips
with Gorgonzola Cheese Dip

SERVES 3 TO 4

Think nachos but made with kettle chips, bacon, sour cream, and Gorgonzola instead of Cheddar. It's decadence on a whole new level. When I made them for my photo shoot, we could barely get them shot before everyone was reaching for a taste. They were gone before I knew it! This is the perfect snack food for sports fans and couch potatoes alike.

1 cup heavy cream

8 ounces crumbled Gorgonzola, divided

4 ounces sour cream

1 tablespoon smoked paprika

1 teaspoon freshly ground black pepper

1 (16-ounce) bag kettle-cooked
   potato chips

1 red bell pepper, seeded and diced

2 pieces cooked bacon, diced

1 bunch chives, chopped

Preheat the oven to 450°F. Line a baking sheet with parchment paper.

In a small saucepan, bring cream to a boil over medium-high heat. Reduce heat to low and simmer about 4 minutes. Stir in about three-quarters of the Gorgonzola, and the sour cream, paprika, and pepper and stir until smooth. Reserve the rest of the cheese for topping.

Place as many potato chips as will fit in a single layer on the prepared baking sheet. Pour about one-third of the cheese sauce over the chips and sprinkle with about one-third of the red pepper and bacon. Continue to layer the chips and cheese mixture until all the ingredients are used.

Bake for 5 to 7 minutes. Remove from oven and sprinkle with the chives and reserved Gorganzola crumbles. Serve warm.

FRYING *on the* FLY

Honestly, I try to eat healthy, but there are times when I crave something fried and deliciously crunchy (especially after a few cocktails). Blame it on the alcohol, but no matter when you have them, these fun-to-eat foods are undeniably comforting to the soul, chile. These recipes are bound to have you going in for seconds, so just don't forget to hit that gym!

Jalapeño Cheese Hush Puppies

SERVES 4

Growing up, "Fish Fry Friday" was a family tradition. I always looked forward to my mom's crispy and golden hush puppies. There is nothing quiet about these puppies because they pack quite a bite! I added a spicy twist with bits of jalapeños and plenty of cheese to this traditional finger food that pairs perfectly with seafood and poultry. You can also take them for a dip in a creamy ranch dressing.

Peanut or vegetable oil, for frying

1 large egg

1 cup buttermilk

1 cup yellow cornmeal

¾ cup all-purpose flour

1 teaspoon baking powder

1 teaspoon kosher salt

1 tablespoon granulated sugar

¼ cup chopped scallions
(about 4 scallions, trimmed)

1 small jalapeño pepper, seeded and minced

1 cup shredded sharp Cheddar

Heat the oil in a deep-fryer or large, heavy pot to 375°F.

Combine all the remaining ingredients in a large bowl. Use an ice-cream scoop to form balls of batter. In batches of three or four at a time, place the balls into the hot oil.

Fry for 4 to 5 minutes, until golden brown. Drain on paper towels.

Tip: Let these get a rich, deep golden color before pulling them out of the oil for good. Check on them and maybe give it a minute or two longer than you think. You can thank me later! It's also fun to slice the peppers and fry up some rings of jalapeño for the side.

Coconut Shrimp *with* Spicy Orange Sauce

MAKES ABOUT 16 TO 20 SHRIMP

If you can't make it to the islands, then bring the islands home to you! No need to travel thousands of miles to savor the sweet and nutty taste of coconut paired with succulent jumbo shrimp when you can make them in your very own kitchen. Just be prepared to see them go fast because they're a real crowd-pleaser. This recipe is simple to prepare and tastes amazing.

SPICY ORANGE SAUCE

1 tablespoon olive oil

1 small shallot, minced

2 garlic cloves, minced

½ cup orange marmalade

¼ cup white wine vinegar

1 tablespoon sriracha

Juice of 1 lemon

SHRIMP

Peanut or vegetable oil, for frying

½ cup all-purpose flour

1 tablespoon chili powder

1 teaspoon onion powder

1 teaspoon freshly ground black pepper

2 large eggs

½ cup panko bread crumbs

2 cups sweetened shredded coconut

1 pound jumbo shrimp, peeled and
    butterflied with tail on

½ teaspoon kosher salt

Prepare the sauce: Heat the olive oil in a saucepan over medium-high heat. Add the shallot and garlic and sauté for 2 to 3 minutes. Add the orange marmalade, white wine vinegar, and sriracha and cook, stirring, for an additional minute. Lower the heat to low and allow the sauce to cook for 5 minutes. Stir in the lemon juice and set aside.

Prepare the shrimp: In a deep, heavy pot or deep-fryer, heat the oil to 350°F.

Line up three medium bowls. In the first bowl, combine the flour, chili powder, onion powder, and pepper. Whisk the eggs together in the second bowl. Stir together the panko bread crumbs and coconut in the third bowl. Dredge the shrimp in the flour mixture first, then in the egg, then in the bread crumb mixture.

In batches of five at a time, place the shrimp in the hot oil and fry until golden brown, 3 to 5 minutes. Sprinkle kosher salt over the shrimp directly out of the fryer.

Serve immediately with the sauce on the side for dipping.

Tip: Sprinkle a pinch of red pepper flakes into your sauce for an added kick of flavor.

Panko-Crusted Soft-Shell Crabs
with Ginger Garlic Sauce

MAKES 4 CRABS

These crabs are one of my favorite things to eat. The meat is extremely flavorful and juicy, bursting from the crusty shell. I use panko bread crumbs because they create a perfectly golden and crispy look with a light taste that brings out the natural flavor of the rich and sweet crab. These are great with the spicy ginger garlic sauce.

GINGER GARLIC SAUCE

2 garlic cloves, minced

1 tablespoon minced fresh ginger

1 teaspoon raw honey

½ cup soy sauce

Zest and juice of 1 lemon, divided

1 tablespoon rice vinegar

2 teaspoons sesame oil

1½ tablespoons unsalted butter

SOFT-SHELL CRABS

Peanut or vegetable oil, for frying

4 fresh soft-shell crabs

1 large egg

Pink Himalayan salt

Freshly ground black pepper

1 cup panko bread crumbs

½ teaspoon paprika

Pinch of cayenne pepper

½ teaspoon lemon pepper

½ bunch parsley, for garnish

1 lemon wedge, for garnish

Prepare the sauce: Whisk together the garlic, ginger, honey, soy sauce, lemon juice, vinegar, and sesame oil in a small bowl.

Melt the butter in a small saucepan over medium heat and add the lemon zest. Allow the butter to brown, 1 minute. Add the garlic mixture to the saucepan and bring to a boil. This will allow all the flavors to marry. Remove from the heat and set aside.

Prepare the crabs: Pour oil into a deep fryer or cast-iron skillet, at least 3 inches deep. Heat oil to 375°F.

Rinse the crabs thoroughly with cold water and pat dry thoroughly with paper towels.

In a shallow bowl, beat the egg and season with pinch each of the salt and pepper. Set aside.

Pour the bread crumbs onto a flat surface or platter. Season with the paprika, a pinch each of the salt, pepper, cayenne, and lemon pepper.

When you're ready to cook the crabs, dip them into the egg mixture one at a time, turning over if necessary. Once the crab is coated with the egg mixture, dip it into the bread crumb mixture. Ensure that the crab is fully coated. You can set aside the crabs until they are all coated and ready to fry.

When the oil is hot, place each crab into the pan so that it is fully submerged. Fry for 3 to 5 minutes, flipping as needed, until crab turns slightly red, and the coating is golden and crisp. You'll probably have to do this in batches.

While crabs are frying, line a plate or platter with paper towels.

When crab is cooked, remove with tongs or a mesh strainer. Allow excess oil to drain back into the pan. Place crab on paper towels. Repeat process with all the crabs, making sure the oil comes back to temperature in between batches.

Serve the crabs with the sauce, rewarmed if necessary, and garnish with the parsley and lemon wedges.

Tip: If you are unfamiliar with cleaning soft-shell crab, or any fish, just ask the seafood service person while at your local fish market and they will happily clean the crabs for you!

Fried Green Tomatoes *with* Cajun Rémoulade

SERVES 4 TO 6

These have long been a family favorite because they are just that good. If you want some variety, you can make fried okra the same way (see variation), or split the recipe between okra and tomatoes, or double up on one of the vegetables. Both have a slightly bitter taste that is complemented with a sweet and spicy rémoulade. Go ahead and rock with it!

CAJUN RÉMOULADE

1 cup mayonnaise

1 tablespoon horseradish

1 tablespoon cider vinegar

Juice of 1 lemon

2 tablespoons Cajun seasoning

1 scallion, trimmed and finely chopped

TOMATOES

Peanut or vegetable oil, for frying

2 pounds green tomatoes (4 to 6 tomatoes), sliced into ¼-inch rounds

SPICE BLEND

½ teaspoon chili powder

½ teaspoon freshly ground black pepper

¼ teaspoon garlic powder

¼ teaspoon kosher salt

1 cup self-rising flour

WET MIXTURE

3 large eggs, beaten

½ cup buttermilk

COATING

½ cup panko bread crumbs

1 cup yellow cornmeal

Prepare the rémoulade: Combine all the rémoulade ingredients in a small bowl. Set aside until ready to serve.

Fill a deep-fryer or large, heavy pot two-thirds of the way (no more than that) with the oil and heat to 350°F.

Lay tomato slices out on a plate, and prepare a dredging station: Lining up three rimmed dishes, mix the spice blend in the first dish, the eggs and buttermilk in the second dish, and the panko and cornmeal in the third dish. Place both sides of each tomato in the spice blend first, then in the wet mixture, and then in the coating.

Place the dredged tomatoes in the hot oil. Fry until golden brown on both sides, flipping after about 30 seconds on the first side.

Transfer the fried tomatoes to a cooling rack or paper towels to drain.

Serve on a large platter with the rémoulade.

Variation: Fried Okra with Cajun Rémoulade

When you talk about the South, you have to talk about okra. Many may be worried by the ooey-gooeyness or the natural "stickiness," but I promise you that this Southern classic will become a family favorite. Following the recipe, simply replace the tomatoes with about 2 pounds of okra, sliced into ½-inch pieces.

Salmon Croquettes *with* Creole Mustard Sauce

MAKES 21 SMALL PATTIES

This is the dish I wanted to learn growing up because I knew my father loved it. It felt like magic, the way my mother would take a few cans of fish and turn them into these crispy patties of deliciousness. She would serve it with hot butter biscuits and Delta syrup. You can try using all salmon, but mackerel adds another dimension. I give mine a Cajun twist since they're so popular among people from the South—and it's a way to sneak in a bit of extra spice!

CREOLE MUSTARD SAUCE

½ cup Dijon mustard

1 teaspoon ground white pepper

3 tablespoons fresh lemon juice

2 teaspoons grapeseed oil

1 teaspoon kosher salt

2 tablespoons honey

CROQUETTES

1 (15-ounce) can salmon, drained, rinsed, picked through and any bones removed

1 (15-ounce) can mackerel, drained, rinsed, picked through and any bones removed

½ cup yellow cornmeal

½ cup all-purpose flour

2 large eggs, beaten

1 tablespoon Worcestershire sauce

1 yellow onion, finely chopped

1 green bell pepper, seeded and finely chopped

1 teaspoon red pepper flakes

2 teaspoons Cajun seasoning

1 teaspoon kosher salt

½ teaspoon freshly ground white pepper

Peanut or vegetable oil, for frying

Prepare the sauce: Whisk together all the sauce ingredients in a small bowl.

Prepare the croquettes: Combine the salmon, mackerel, cornmeal, flour, eggs, Worcestershire, onion, bell pepper, red pepper flakes, Cajun seasoning, salt, and pepper in a large bowl. Mix well by hand.

Heat the oil, at least 2 inches deep, in a large cast-iron skillet over high heat until it reaches 350°F on a thermometer. Line a baking sheet with paper towels.

Using the palm of your hand, form patties from the fish mixture. Place three to four patties into the oil and allow to fry for 5 minutes or until golden brown and crunchy on the outside and cooked evenly throughout. Remove the patties using a slotted spoon to the paper towel-lined baking sheet and season with additional salt. Repeat with remaining patties.

Serve patties hot, with the sauce on the side.

Tip: You can cut the recipe in half if you want, but if you can't find a smaller can of mackerel, just use half, or use all salmon.

Salmon Croquettes

"When I was about 12 years old, I already felt like a sous chef thanks to spending so much time with my mother in the kitchen, assisting her with the chopping and dicing, as well as the frying and the grilling. Well, at this point in my life, I had this great idea to make something special for my dad. I knew that he loved salmon croquettes and I planned to make them for him, just like my mother did.

So, I opened up the cans of mackerel and salmon and diced the peppers and onions just like my mother taught me. I formed the patties and carefully placed them in the hot oil. My croquettes were turning a beautiful golden brown, just like my mom's, and I just knew that my dad was going to love them.

Girl, bye!

My dad sat there looking at his croquettes and he was skinnin' and grinnin' from ear-to-ear. "Oh Pumpkin, this looks delicious!" he said. He took a bite and then he looked at me with a puzzled look on his face. "Pumpkin, these are delicious, but I think that your mom removes the bones!"

Dang! While watching my mom prepare this dish many times, I must not have noticed this essential step in preparing the recipe. This silly mistake ruined what I thought were the best croquettes ever.

Even though I was so disappointed in myself, my father never made me feel bad. He struggled through his meal and ate those croquettes like they were the best thing since color television.

Looking back many years later, I dubbed them the "struggle croquettes," and I never forgot that step again.

TIP: Remove the bones from the salmon and mackerel before forming into patties.

Buffalo Chicken Lettuce Wraps

When I'm looking for an easy crowd-pleaser that is not only delicious, but also appealing to look at, these lettuce wraps are my top choice. The presentation of the hot and spicy chicken served on Bibb lettuce is special enough for any occasion. Serve them open-faced and let the good times roll.

BUFFALO SAUCE

½ cup hot sauce

1 tablespoon Worcestershire sauce

3 tablespoons unsalted butter

BUFFALO CHICKEN

1 pound boneless, skinless chicken breasts

¼ cup hot sauce

2 teaspoons Dijon mustard

Peanut or vegetable oil, for frying

1 cup all-purpose flour

2 tablespoons paprika

½ teaspoon cayenne pepper (optional)

1 teaspoon freshly ground black pepper

1 teaspoon onion powder

1 cup blue cheese crumbles

½ cup shredded carrots

Bibb lettuce, separated into 8 leaves

Prepare the sauce: Combine all the sauce ingredients in a small saucepan over low heat and heat until the butter is completely melted. Remove from the heat and set aside.

Prepare the chicken: Cut the chicken breasts into 1-inch cubes. Combine the cubed chicken, hot sauce, and Dijon in a large bowl, toss to evenly coat, and set aside.

Pour enough oil into a large skillet to reach 2 to 3 inches deep. Place over medium-high heat.

Combine the flour, paprika, cayenne (if using), pepper, and onion powder in a shallow bowl. Dredge the cubed chicken in the flour mixture, then dust off any excess flour.

Once the oil is at 375°F, it's ready. Place the chicken in the oil and fry for 2 to 3 minutes per side, until the chicken is golden brown and crispy. Transfer the cooked chicken to a cooling rack or paper towels to drain any excess oil.

Toss the chicken with the Buffalo sauce to coat evenly.

Serve immediately on a platter with the blue cheese crumbles, shredded carrots, and Bibb lettuce. Allow guests to build their wraps. Season to taste with salt and pepper.

Crispy Chicken Sliders

MAKES 12 SLIDERS

Planning on entertaining a few friends? My crispy sliders are just what you need! They boast my signature crunchy coated chicken that ensures a moist and juicy center. Serve with a side of blue cheese dressing for a special touch, or if you're feeling daring, add a little bit of my spicy mayo for a dynamic kick.

SRIRACHA MAYONNAISE

1 cup mayonnaise

3 tablespoons sriracha

SLIDERS

1 cup all-purpose flour

1 cup buttermilk

¼ cup hot sauce

1 tablespoon Worcestershire sauce

Peanut or vegetable oil, for frying

2½ pounds boneless, skinless chicken breasts, cut into strips

1 tablespoon Creole seasoning

12 of your favorite slider buns (I prefer Pepperidge Farm Sweet & Soft)

Romaine lettuce (optional)

Pepper Jack or provolone (optional)

Prepare the sriracha mayonnaise: Combine mayonnaise and sriracha in a small bowl, cover with plastic wrap, and refrigerate.

Prepare the sliders: Combine the flour, buttermilk, hot sauce, and Worcestershire sauce in a medium bowl.

Pour enough oil into a large skillet to reach 2 to 3 inches deep. Place over medium-high heat.

Meanwhile, sprinkle the chicken with the Creole seasoning. Dip into the flour mixture to coat.

Once the oil is at 375°F, it's ready. Place the chicken in the oil and fry for 4 to 5 minutes per side, until the chicken is golden brown and crispy and registers 160°F on a meat thermometer.

To assemble the sliders: Spread the sriracha mayo inside the top and bottom of the buns and nestle the chicken in between. Add romaine lettuce and pepper Jack or provolone, if desired.

GOING GREEN:
Starring SALADS!

Salads are normally considered the sidekick to a meal, but trust me when I say these salads are so flavorful and fancy that they become the star of the show! I promise you, hunni, these salads are everything solo—especially if you're like me and are constantly on the go!

BLT Salad with Chunky Blue Cheese Dressing   79

Turkey Spring Salad with Creamy Cajun Dressing   82

Cucumber, Broccoli, and Tomato Salad with
Chili Lime Vinaigrette   83

Shredded Cabbage Salad with Apples and
Sliced Almonds   85

Peach, Fig, and Arugula Salad with
Spicy Lemon Honey Vinaigrette   86

Kale Citrus Salad with Honey Goat Cheese and
Tangerine Vinaigrette   89

BLT Salad *with* Chunky Blue Cheese Dressing

SERVES 2 TO 4

If you're in the mood for a BLT sans the bread, this delicious salad has the guts to be served solo, satisfying your appetite. The creamy blue cheese dressing and a boiled egg for additional protein give you a powerful meal, especially for lunch.

BLUE CHEESE DRESSING

4 ounces blue cheese, crumbled, plus additional for topping

½ cup mayonnaise

¼ cup sour cream

Juice of 1 lemon

2 garlic cloves, minced

1 tablespoon minced fresh cilantro

1 tablespoon minced fresh chives

½ teaspoon cayenne pepper

Kosher salt and freshly ground black pepper

SALAD

1 head romaine lettuce, roughly chopped

4 large hard-boiled eggs, halved

3 medium tomatoes, sliced

6 slices crispy bacon, crumbled

Prepare the dressing: Combine all the dressing ingredients in a small bowl, cover with plastic wrap, and refrigerate until ready to serve.

Assemble the salad: Arrange the lettuce in an even layer on a large serving platter.

Add the eggs and tomatoes in a single layer, then top with the chopped bacon.

Serve the dressing on the side.

Note: If dressing is too thick, thin with buttermilk or cream.

Turkey Spring Salad
with Creamy Cajun Dressing

SERVES 2 TO 4

This salad is a meal! I prefer to use delicious Boar's Head Cajun Turkey, along with fresh vegetables to ensure my salad has a delicious crunch. Add a few wontons to really enhance this satisfying dish.

CREAMY CAJUN DRESSING

2 teaspoons Cajun seasoning

1 teaspoon garlic powder

1 teaspoon onion powder

1 teaspoon kosher salt

¼ teaspoon freshly ground black pepper

½ cup sour cream

¼ cup mayonnaise

2 teaspoons cider vinegar

Juice of 1 lemon

SALAD

2 cups spring salad mix

2 cups arugula

2 cups grape tomatoes, halved

2 large carrots, shredded

3 large hard-boiled eggs, halved

1 (15-ounce) can corn, drained

1 pound Cajun-style turkey, sliced (I prefer Boar's Head)

2 scallions, trimmed and chopped

Prepare the dressing: Whisk together all the dressing ingredients in a small bowl. Cover with plastic wrap and refrigerate until ready to serve.

Assemble the salad in layers: First, combine the spring salad mix and arugula and place it in an even layer on a large serving platter. This creates a foundation for the remaining salad ingredients.

Layer the tomatoes, carrot, cucumber, eggs, and corn evenly over the greens. Add the Cajun turkey and scallions across the top. Roll the turkey slices or cut them into strips. You can cut the eggs in half or chop them. Serve the salad layered or tossed.

Serve with the dressing.

Cucumber, Broccoli, *and* Tomato Salad *with* Chili Lime Vinaigrette

SERVES 2 TO 4

Thanks to the limes, this salad has an acidic taste with a hearty crunch that is not only delicious but also very healthy. The secret ingredient is a packet of zesty Italian salad mix. The salty and spicy powder coats the vegetables and keeps them extra-crunchy. You could add cooked beef or pork to this salad, or serve it alongside a hearty meat dish.

CHILI LIME VINAIGRETTE

6 tablespoons olive oil

2 tablespoons red wine vinegar

2 tablespoons honey

1 teaspoon Dijon mustard

Juice of 2 limes

1 teaspoon chili powder

¼ teaspoon dried oregano

¼ teaspoon kosher salt

¼ teaspoon freshly ground black pepper

SALAD

3 English cucumbers, sliced, halved, and seeded

4 broccoli crowns, chopped into florets

3 cups grape tomatoes

1 large red onion, thinly sliced (about ½ cup)

1 (8-ounce) packet of zesty Italian salad dressing mix

Prepare the vinaigrette: Whisk together all the vinaigrette ingredients in a small bowl until completely combined. Cover with plastic wrap and refrigerate until serving.

Prepare the salad: Combine the cucumbers, broccoli, tomatoes, and red onion in a large bowl. Add the Italian salad dressing mix and toss to coat evenly.

Toss the salad with the vinaigrette and serve.

Shredded Cabbage Salad
with Apples *and* Sliced Almonds

SERVES 4 TO 6

If you have 10 minutes, then you have more than enough time to make a salad that tastes like heaven. This sweet and nutty spring salad has the perfect crunch to accompany any meat, especially pork or tender lamb. I add a sweet and sour vinaigrette dressing for a mouthwatering finish.

DRESSING

½ cup olive oil

3 tablespoons cider vinegar

2 tablespoons honey

Juice of 1 lemon

½ teaspoon kosher salt

¼ teaspoon freshly ground black pepper

SALAD

1 small green cabbage, shredded (about 4 to 5 cups)

3 green apples, cored and grated

3 carrots, peeled and shredded

5 scallions, trimmed and thinly chopped

½ cup sliced almonds

Prepare the dressing: Whisk together all the dressing ingredients in a bowl large enough to fit the other ingredients until completely combined.

Add all the salad ingredients and toss with the dressing to coat evenly.

Serve immediately or refrigerate.

Peach, Fig, *and* Arugula Salad *with* Spicy Lemon Honey Vinaigrette

SERVES 2 TO 4

This salad is a celebration of taste and texture. There are juicy peaches and luscious figs tossed with bitter arugula and studded with sweet little pieces of date. The vinaigrette ties it all together with the hit of sriracha and lemon. The chopping and slicing takes a bit of time, but the result is worth it.

VINAIGRETTE

1 garlic clove, minced

Juice of 1 lemon

2 tablespoons honey

1 tablespoon sriracha

¼ teaspoon kosher salt

¾ cup olive oil

SALAD

5 ounces arugula, rinsed and dried

4 peaches, pitted and sliced

8 figs, quartered

⅓ cup pitted dates, coarsely chopped

1 small shallot, thinly sliced

Prepare the vinaigrette: Combine the garlic, lemon juice, honey, sriracha, and salt in a lidded jar. Add the oil and shake well until incorporated.

Assemble the salad: Spread the arugula on a large platter.

Place the peaches, figs, dates, and shallot in a small bowl and toss with about 2 tablespoons of the vinaigrette, then place on top of the arugula.

Serve with remaining vinaigrette.

Kale Citrus Salad *with* Honey Goat Cheese *and* Tangerine Vinaigrette

SERVES 6

This crisp salad is surprisingly sweet, but adds a little sass with vinaigrette tanginess. I love including goat cheese as the special accent because the creamy texture heightens the taste to make a simple salad fit for royalty.

TANGERINE VINAIGRETTE

⅓ cup fresh orange juice

Juice of 2 tangerines

1 teaspoon honey

2 garlic cloves, minced

1 teaspoon Dijon mustard

1 cup olive oil

Salt and freshly ground black pepper

SALAD

1 bunch kale leaves, stemmed

1 tablespoon olive oil

1 teaspoon kosher salt

1 large red onion, sliced

3 oranges, peeled and diced

¼ cup dried cranberries

4 ounces honey goat cheese

Prepare the vinaigrette: Combine the orange and tangerine juices, honey, garlic, and Dijon in a small bowl. Whisk in the oil, and add salt and pepper to taste.

Place the kale in a bowl along with the oil and salt and massage until the leaves soften and become shiny.

Add the red onion, diced oranges, and dried cranberries to the kale, top with the vinaigrette, and toss.

Top the salad with the honey goat cheese. Serve at room temperature.

Forget the Fork: FLAVOR at Your FINGERTIPS

No shade to grandma's pimiento cheese sandwich, but these, my dear, are sassy sandwiches created with the same amount of love yet with a lot more style and sophistication.

Cheesy Baked Hawaiian Roll Sloppy Joes

MAKES 12 SLIDERS

Entertaining a few friends who love sports? This childhood favorite will win big when served while viewing a big game. Simple and easy to make, these cheesy, sloppy sandwiches are best with chips and a cold beer. Be sure to have plenty of napkins available.

1 pound ground beef

3 shallots, diced

1 tablespoon chili powder

¼ teaspoon kosher salt

⅓ teaspoon freshly ground black pepper

1 (16-ounce) can sloppy joe sauce

12 Hawaiian slider buns

1 cup shredded mozzarella

2 tablespoons unsalted butter, melted

1 teaspoon minced garlic

Preheat the oven to 350°F. Line a baking sheet with parchment paper.

Heat a large skillet over medium-low heat. Combine the beef, shallots, chili powder, salt, and pepper in the skillet. Sauté until the beef is browned completely, then drain the beef in a colander.

Transfer the cooked beef to a bowl, add the sloppy joe sauce, and stir until the meat is evenly coated.

Place the bottom halves of the slider buns on the prepared baking sheet, cut side up. Don't bother separating the individual rolls, as it's easier to add the filling when they are attached. Top evenly with the meat mixture, then sprinkle evenly with the cheese. Cover with the top halves of the buns.

Mix the melted butter with the minced garlic and brush the mixture over the tops of the sliders.

Bake for 20 minutes, or until the cheese is melted and the slider buns begin to brown.

Remove from the oven and serve while hot.

Corned Beef *and* Pastrami Reuben

MAKES 4 SANDWICHES

When I think of Friday nights, my mouth instantly waters for a corned beef and pastrami Reuben, probably because this was the sandwich I would often share with my mom as we would catch up on our weekly events and bond over a good meal. I have a feeling that you and your loved ones will also enjoy this sandwich, which is stacked high with savory meat that is not only hearty, but also tasty. Pair it with a kosher pickle, kettle chips, and a cold drink for a delightful weekend kickoff.

1 cup sauerkraut, drained

4 tablespoons (½ stick) unsalted butter, at room temperature

8 slices marble rye bread

1 cup Thousand Island dressing

8 slices Swiss cheese

8 slices thinly shaved pastrami

8 slices thick, deli-sliced corned beef

Heat a flat-top grill or large skillet over medium-low heat.

Spread the butter evenly on one side of each slice of bread. Spread the Thousand Island dressing on the opposite side of each slice of bread.

On the dressing side of each of four bread slices, layer one slice of Swiss cheese, two slices of pastrami, two slices of corn beef, ¼ cup of the sauerkraut mixture, then another slice of Swiss cheese. Top each stack with one of the remaining four slices of bread, buttered side up.

Place all four sandwiches on the grill. Cover the sandwiches with a heatproof lid to allow the cheese to melt, and grill, covered, for about 5 minutes per side, or until the bread is golden brown and the cheese is melted.

Serve immediately while hot.

Monterey Jack Patty Melts
with Caramelized Onion *and* Jalapeño Relish

I always get a thumbs-up when I make this easy, cheesy, and deliciously juicy sandwich. Whether you use ground turkey or 100 percent ground beef for your patty, this burger is served with sweet caramelized onions on Texas toast. Don't forget the homemade relish to add a hit of heat. Yaaassss!

RELISH

3 tablespoons olive oil

2 large yellow onions, sliced

1 cup pickled sliced jalapeño peppers, drained

2 garlic cloves, minced

1 teaspoon adobo seasoning

¼ teaspoon freshly ground black pepper

¼ cup brown sugar

PATTIES

1 pound ground beef (see Note)

2 tablespoons Worcestershire sauce

1 teaspoon cayenne pepper

½ teaspoon kosher salt

1 teaspoon freshly ground black pepper

½ teaspoon garlic powder

TO ASSEMBLE

4 tablespoons (½ stick) unsalted butter, at room temperature

8 slices Texas toast, or other thick-cut soft bread

8 slices Monterey Jack

Prepare the relish: Heat a flat-top grill or large skillet over medium-low heat. Heat the oil. Add the onions, jalapeños, garlic, adobo, and black pepper and sauté for 5 minutes, or until the onions begin to brown. Add the brown sugar and sauté for 10 minutes, or until the onions and jalapeños are caramelized. Remove from the grill and set aside, leaving the grill on the stovetop

Prepare the patties: Combine the beef, Worcestershire, cayenne, salt, black pepper, and garlic powder in a bowl. Mix together until the seasoning is completely incorporated into the meat. Divide the meat into four equal patties.

Place the beef patties on the grill and cook until browned on both sides, about 5 minutes per side. Remove the patties from the grill and allow to rest on a cooling rack or plate.

Clean the grill and reheat over medium-low heat.

Spread the butter on one side of each slice of bread. On the unbuttered side of each of four bread slices, layer one slice of cheese, one beef patty, the relish, and another slice of cheese, then top each stack with the another slice of bread, buttered side up.

Place the four sandwiches on the grill and cover with a heatproof lid to allow the cheese to melt. Grill for 3 to 5 minutes per side, until golden brown on each side and the cheese is melted.

Slice the patty melts in half. Serve immediately.

Note: Replace ground beef with ground turkey, if desired.

Cheddar BBQ Turkey Burgers

MAKES 4 TO 6 BURGERS

This is one of my favorite turkey burger recipes due to the melody of flavors that dance on your tongue with every bite. My sweet and tangy sauce topped with seriously sharp cheese, grilled red onions, and poblano peppers make the perfect burger. To up the ante, pair it with my tasty Spicy Mustard Slaw (page 103) and you will leave the table full and satisfied. These are large burgers, so feel free to make more patties if you want to.

PEPPERS AND ONIONS

4 whole poblano peppers, seeded and halved

1 large red onion, sliced

1 tablespoon olive oil

BURGERS

2 pounds ground turkey

2 tablespoons Worcestershire sauce

1 teaspoon paprika

1 teaspoon ground cumin

1 teaspoon dried sage

1 teaspoon garlic powder

1 teaspoon kosher salt

1 teaspoon freshly ground black pepper

1 large egg, beaten

2 tablespoons olive oil

TO ASSEMBLE

4 to 6 brioche hamburger buns, split and toasted

4 to 6 slices extra sharp Cheddar

Mayonnaise

BBQ sauce (see page 100)

Lettuce

Tomato

Red Onion

Guacamole (optional)

Prepare the peppers and onions: Preheat oven to 425°F. Place the peppers, cut side down, on one side of a roasting pan. Spread the onion slices on the other half. Drizzle everything with about 1 tablespoon olive oil. Roast for 7 to 10 minutes, or until soft. The skin of the peppers should darken and shimmer. Set aside. You can also roast these on your grill pan or skillet, but the oven softens them up more.

Prepare the burgers: Combine all the ingredients, except the oil, in a large bowl. Mix well until the seasonings and egg are completely incorporated with the turkey. Divide the mixture into four to six patties.

Heat a grill pan or large skillet over medium heat.

Pour 2 tablespoons of the oil into the pan and heat. Add the patties and cook for 5 to 8 minutes on each side, until completely cooked, without any pink. Place a slice of Cheddar on top of each burger and cover with a heatproof lid to allow the cheese to melt, 2 to 3 minutes.

Assemble the burgers: Spread the mayonnaise evenly on the bottom half of each bun, then top with burger, a portion of sautéed onions, roasted poblano peppers, lettuce, tomato, red onion, BBQ sauce, and guacamole, if using. Cover with top bun and serve immediately.

Memphis BBQ Pulled Pork Sliders

MAKES 12 SLIDERS

Hunni, when it comes to pork, Memphis is the place to be, hands down! I created these pulled pork sliders to be sweet and savory, especially with the juicy and flavorful slow-cooked meat. If you're planning to cook the pork especially for this dish, you'll need to set aside enough time for marinating and cooking as described on page 196. Add my tangy BBQ sauce to the cooked pork and pass the extra.

BBQ SAUCE

2 tablespoons unsalted butter

1 small onion, finely chopped

2 garlic cloves, minced

2 cups ketchup

½ cup cider vinegar

⅓ cup molasses

2 tablespoons Worcestershire sauce

3 tablespoons brown sugar

2 tablespoons granulated sugar

2 teaspoons dried mustard

1 teaspoon kosher salt

1 teaspoon freshly ground black pepper

¼ teaspoon red pepper flakes

Juice of 1 lemon

SLIDERS

2 pounds pulled pork (see Memphis BBQ Pulled Pork, page 196)

12 of your favorite slider buns (I prefer Pepperidge Farm Sweet & Savory)

Spicy Mustard Slaw (page 103) or prepared coleslaw

Thick-cut pickles

Preheat the oven to 300°F.

Prepare the BBQ sauce: Melt the butter in large saucepan over medium heat.

Sauté onion and garlic for about 5 minutes, until garlic is browned but not crispy. Stir in the rest of the ingredients, except for the lemon juice.

Turn the heat up to medium-high and bring to a boil, whisking to keep sauce from sticking to pan. Once you've reached a rolling boil, reduce heat to low and cover. Let simmer for 25 minutes, stirring occasionally.

While the sauce is cooking, warm the pulled pork: Place 2 pounds of cooked pulled pork into an oven-proof pan and warm until steaming, 15 to 20 minutes. Remove the pork from the oven and, if desired, warm the slider buns for 5 to 10 minutes.

When the sauce has thickened, move it off the heat and quickly stir in the lemon juice. Pour about a cup of BBQ sauce over the pulled pork and toss to coat thoroughly. Use more or less as desired.

Prepare the sliders: Remove buns from oven if you've warmed them and place them open-faced onto a platter. Place generous amounts of pulled pork on the base of the slider buns, top with extra sauce, slaw, and a pickle. Serve warm.

Note: Lemon juice really brightens up any barbecue sauce. If you buy store-bought BBQ sauce, stir in a splash or two of fresh lemon juice just before serving for a nice pop of freshness.

Thick-Cut Fried Bologna Sandwiches *with* Spicy Mustard Slaw

MAKES 4 SANDWICHES

This sandwich is a down-home favorite that's served in almost every bar in Tennessee. It is made on buttered Texas toast with a spicy mustard slaw that tones down the saltiness of the meat. As a plus, this slaw tastes great with any of my sandwiches—just keep your leftovers refrigerated and add to all sandwiches that are passing through your kitchen.

MUSTARD DRESSING

¼ cup yellow mustard (see Note)

¼ cup mayonnaise

4 teaspoons cider vinegar

2 teaspoons cayenne pepper, or more to taste

2 teaspoons granulated sugar

¼ teaspoon kosher salt

SLAW

½ small green cabbage, cored and shredded (about 2 cups)

2 whole carrots, peeled and shredded (about 1 cup)

SANDWICHES

2 tablespoons vegetable oil, plus more as needed

12 slices thick-cut bologna

2 tablespoons unsalted butter, plus more as needed

8 slices Texas Toast or other thick-cut soft bread

½ cup stone-ground mustard, plus more as needed (see Note)

16 kosher dill sandwich slices

Prepare the mustard dressing and slaw: In a mixing bowl, combine the dressing ingredients. Fold in cabbage and carrots and toss until vegetables are evenly coated. Set aside.

Prepare the sandwiches: Preheat a large skillet to medium-low heat. Heat about 2 tablespoons vegetable oil, enough to coat the bottom of the skillet, until shimmering. Fry the bologna until browned, about 3 minutes per side. Cook in batches, adding oil as needed. Remove the bologna and set aside. Wipe out skillet.

Melt about 2 tablespoons butter in skillet over medium heat. Fry each piece of bread on one side until golden brown, about 3 minutes. Work in batches, adding more butter as needed. Remove from skillet and lay bread, buttered side down, on clean plates.

Spread mustard evenly on both slices of bread. For each sandwich, layer one slice of bread with three slices of fried bologna folded in half, kosher dill sandwich slices, and slaw. Top with remaining bread slice.

Serve immediately.

Note: I always have yellow and stone-ground mustards on hand, but you can use either one for the slaw and the sandwich.

Brown Butter Lobster Rolls
with Sriracha Mayo

MAKES 4 LOBSTER ROLLS

There are times when you just have to treat yourself to something delectable, and this right here will have you wanting to kiss yourself! A snack that a chef can admire, this succulent and tender lobster is sweet and pairs well with the creamy and spicy sriracha mayo. Place the lobster on a buttery roll and let the divine dining experience begin. Add a twist of lemon on the side for garnish and enjoy because you deserve it!

LOBSTER

2 tablespoons unsalted butter, melted

Juice of 1 lemon

¼ teaspoon kosher salt

⅛ teaspoon freshly ground black pepper

2 lobster tails or ¾ pound cooked lobster meat

SRIRACHA MAYONNAISE

½ cup mayonnaise

1 tablespoon sriracha, or more to taste

TO ASSEMBLE

4 top-split buns

3 tablespoons chopped fresh chives, to garnish

Stir together the butter, lemon juice, salt, and pepper in a small bowl until completely combined.

If using cooked lobster meat, cut into small chunks and toss with lemon butter.

If using lobster tails, prepare them now: Preheat oven to 425°F. Coat an oven-safe pan evenly with nonstick cooking spray. Place the tails, meat side up, in the prepared pan. Spread 2 tablespoons of the butter mixture evenly on the meat of both lobster tails.

Roast in the oven for 5 to 8 minutes, until the lobster meat is opaque. Remove each tail from its shell and chop into bite-size pieces.

Prepare the sriracha mayonnaise: Mix mayonnaise and sriracha. Spread mayo thickly on buns. Stuff the buns with the lobster meat and top with more sriracha mayo, if desired, and chives. Serve immediately while hot.

Seductive Sides: VEGETABLES to DEVOUR

Don't tell me you don't like vegetables! Mine are spiced just right, and often include bacon or smoked turkey. These dishes will blow your mind. Now go ahead and eat your veggies.

Sautéed Lemon-Garlic Asparagus

SERVES 4

When I am in need of a quick side dish, I go for this simple but tasty take on regular old asparagus. The garlic is perfectly balanced with a twist of lemon, and the grilled slices of citrus add an extra pop of color and sophistication.

3 tablespoons olive oil

2 pounds fresh asparagus, ends trimmed

¼ teaspoon kosher salt

¼ teaspoon freshly ground black pepper

2 garlic cloves, minced

Juice of 1 lemon

Sautéed lemons, for garnish (see Tip)

Heat the oil in a large skillet or grill pan over medium-high heat. Add the asparagus, salt, and pepper and sauté until crisp-tender, 3 to 4 minutes. Add the garlic and sauté for an additional minute.

Add more salt and pepper to taste and the lemon juice, toss to combine, and plate on a large platter. If using sautéed lemon (see tip), add now.

Tip: Sautéed lemon slices make a beautiful addition to this dish. Wash and scrub one lemon, then cut into thin slices. After cooking the asparagus, wipe out the skillet and heat over medium-high heat. Toss the lemon slices in the pan until slightly caramelized. Transfer to the platter for added flavor and presentation.

Southern Turnip Greens

SERVES 4

One of the most significant differences between turnip greens and all of the other greens is that the turnip green is a bit more tender. I cook it a little longer so the leaves can really soak up the seasonings, creating a delectable taste with every bite. You're gonna love my recipe that includes onions, hot sauce, and smoked turkey because it is not only tasty but healthy and delicious.

4 cups water

1¼ teaspoons kosher salt, divided

3 medium turnips, peeled and
    cut into 1-inch cubes

2 tablespoons olive oil

1 yellow onion, diced

1 pound turnip greens, cleaned and
    chopped

1 smoked turkey wing

4 cups chicken stock

2 tablespoons cider vinegar

1 tablespoon hot sauce

¼ teaspoon freshly ground black
    pepper

2 large tomatoes, sliced

1 yellow onion, sliced

Bring the water and 1 teaspoon salt to a boil in a medium pot over medium-high heat. Add the turnips and cook for 40 minutes, or until fork-tender. Drain the turnips and set aside.

Heat the oil in a heavy-bottomed stockpot over medium-high heat. Add the diced onion and sauté until translucent.

Add the turnip greens, smoked turkey wing, chicken stock, vinegar, hot sauce, ¼ teaspoon salt, and pepper to the pot. Cover the pot and bring to a boil, then reduce the heat to medium-low and allow the greens to simmer for 1½ hours, or until tender.

Remove turkey wing from the pot. Pick the meat off the bone and add back to the pot. Add turnip bottoms to the pot and stir until combined.

Serve hot with sliced tomatoes and onion.

Spiced Oven-Roasted Cauliflower

SERVES 4

*When I tell you that roasted cauliflower is the simplest side you can make, I tell you the truth!
Whether you cook it as a steak, popcorn, or roasted whole, add a little seasoning, pop it in the
oven, and enjoy. Cauliflower will always be the side dish for the win.*

1 large head cauliflower, cut into florets

4 tablespoons olive oil, divided

1 tablespoon chili powder

2 teaspoons kosher salt

½ teaspoon freshly ground black
pepper

¼ teaspoon ground turmeric

2 tablespoons chopped parsley

Preheat the oven to 450°F.

Combine the cauliflower with 3 tablespoons of the oil and
the chili powder, salt, pepper, and turmeric in a bowl until
evenly coated.

Line a baking sheet with parchment paper and coat with
remaining tablespoon of oil. Spread the cauliflower in
a single layer on prepared baking sheet. Roast until the
edges begin to char, 12 to 15 minutes.

Sprinkle with parsley and serve immediately.

Note: I like my cauliflower on the crispy side of cooked. If
you prefer yours softer inside, increase cooking time to 20
to 25 minutes.

COOKING WITH *Miss Quad*

Smothered Cabbage

SERVES 6 TO 8

Cooked right, cabbage is one of the most melt-in-your-mouth tasty vegetables you could ever eat. This recipe calls for you to smother the cabbage, to cook it slowly while it absorbs the accents of garlic, red pepper flakes, and butter. I use shredded carrots and red bell pepper for color, and add potato to create a comforting and nourishing dish.

8 small golden potatoes (about 1 pound), peeled and halved

2 tablespoons unsalted butter

3 garlic cloves, minced

1 large green cabbage, cored and chopped (6 to 8 cups)

2 yellow onions, diced

1 medium carrot, peeled and shredded (about ½ cup)

2 bell peppers, seeded and thinly sliced (I use red and orange)

½ teaspoon crushed red pepper flakes (see Note)

½ teaspoon kosher salt

¼ teaspoon freshly ground black pepper

¼ cup chicken stock, plus more if needed

In a large stock pot over medium-high heat, bring 8 quarts of water to a rolling boil. Add the halved potatoes and boil uncovered for 10 to 20 minutes, or until a knife pierces them easily. Remove from the heat, drain, and set aside.

Melt 1 tablespoon of the butter in a large Dutch oven over medium-high heat. Add garlic and sauté until fragrant, about 2 minutes. Stir in remaining ingredients.

Reduce heat to medium-low and stir in remaining butter. Cover pot with lid, and simmer for 40 minutes or until cabbage is tender. If mixture seems dry, add more chicken stock, ¼ cup at a time.

Before serving, stir in potatoes. Cover and simmer for 5 additional minutes, or until potatoes are warmed through. Serve immediately.

Note: I like my food really spicy, so I add three to four times more red pepper than I call for in this recipe. Don't be afraid to add more to taste!

Sautéed Green Beans
with Crispy Bacon *and* Shallots

SERVES 4 TO 6

I made these for Thanksgiving and the crowd went wild! Since then, I've discovered how popular they are at any time of the year. Using fresh green beans, I cook them just enough to be tender inside but still firm outside. I add a little salt and shallots, and to top off the taste, I add crispy and smoky bacon, which makes this a side dish that is always devoured. Soy sauce adds a nice, salty complexity.

6 slices thick-cut bacon, diced

2 large shallots, minced

2 pounds green beans, ends trimmed

1 tablespoon soy sauce

Kosher salt

Heat a large skillet over medium-high heat. Add the bacon and shallots and sauté until the bacon is crispy. Remove from the skillet with a slotted spoon and allow to drain on a paper towel.

Add the green beans to the pan and sauté in the bacon fat for 5 to 8 minutes. Remove from the skillet and drain on a paper towel. Discard the remaining bacon fat from the skillet.

Pour the soy sauce into the skillet and add back the green beans, shallots, and bacon. Toss to combine. Taste and add salt, if needed.

Serve immediately.

Soy Ginger Veggie Stir-Fry

SERVES 2

One day I had a yearning for mouthwatering Chinese food, so I decided to try making my own. Honestly, I was so surprised by the taste and flavor that I had to share this recipe with you. I make it a point to add fresh and healthy vegetables, so this stir-fry has not only a brilliant color, but also a great crunch. To make the meal filling, serve over a bed of jasmine rice or soba noodles and you can't go wrong! You can also add a little tofu, shrimp, or chicken for protein.

3 tablespoons olive oil

¼ cup soy sauce

½ red onion, chopped

½ cup snow peas

½ cup chopped bok choy

½ cup fresh broccoli florets

¼ cup julienned zucchini

½ cup canned baby corn, drained

1 carrot, shredded

1 small red chili pepper, diced

3 tablespoons minced garlic

1 teaspoon kosher salt

1 teaspoon freshly ground black pepper

2 tablespoons unsalted butter

1 teaspoon minced fresh ginger

1 teaspoon honey

Cooked jasmine rice or soba noodles, for serving

Combine the oil, soy sauce, red onion, snow peas, bok choy, broccoli, zucchini, baby corn, carrot, and red chili pepper in a large bowl. Mix well, making sure all the vegetables are coated. Add the garlic, salt, and black pepper, and toss well. Set aside.

Melt the butter in a large wok over medium-high heat, about 2 minutes. Add the ginger and sauté for 2 minutes. This will give a maximum flavor profile to coat the veggie mixture. Stir in the honey, and then all the vegetables.

Stir-fry the vegetables over medium-high heat for 4 to 6 minutes, using a large spatula, making sure that you are evenly rotating the contents around the wok.

Remove from the heat, and serve immediately with jasmine rice or soba noodles.

Creamed Corn *with* Corn Bread Crust

SERVES 8 TO 10

This dish is a childhood favorite of mine that I loved to eat with almost any meal. I find that the corn bread crust looks a bit like a cake, which makes this favorite veggie more like a dessert. Pop it in the oven and watch this beauty turn golden brown. Serve with my Pecan Crusted Trout (see page 159) to ensure a delightful meal that your whole family will enjoy!

⅔ cup all-purpose flour

½ cup yellow cornmeal

⅓ cup granulated sugar

2 teaspoons baking powder

1 teaspoon baking soda

½ teaspoon kosher salt

½ cup sour cream

8 tablespoons (1 stick) unsalted butter, melted

2 tablespoons vegetable oil

2 large eggs, beaten

¼ teaspoon vanilla extract

2 (14-ounce) cans creamed corn

1 (14-ounce) can corn kernels, drained

Preheat the oven to 350°F. Spray a 9-by-13-inch casserole dish with nonstick cooking spray and set aside.

Combine the flour, cornmeal, sugar, baking powder, baking soda, and salt in a large bowl.

In a separate medium bowl, combine the sour cream, melted butter, oil, eggs, and vanilla.

Gently fold the wet ingredients into dry until completely combined. Add the creamed corn and corn kernels and mix until completely combined.

Pour the mixture, in an even layer, into the prepared casserole dish. Bake for 40 to 50 minutes, or until golden brown. Stick a toothpick into the center to test whether the corn bread is completely cooked. If the toothpick comes out clean, remove the casserole from the oven and allow it to rest for 8 to 10 minutes.

Serve warm.

Roasted Brussels Sprouts

SERVES 2 TO 4

Many people get a frown on their face at the thought of Brussels sprouts because of their childhood experiences with them. Hunni, these are not your mama's Brussels sprouts. The natural bite of these gems is mellowed when roasted with olive oil and flavored with kosher salt and ground black pepper. I take it up a notch by adding minced garlic and shallots for a fresh taste. Go ahead and try them. I promise you won't regret it.

1 pound fresh Brussels sprouts, halved lengthwise

1 large shallot, diced

4 garlic cloves

3 tablespoons olive oil

1 teaspoon kosher salt

½ teaspoon freshly ground black pepper

½ teaspoon red pepper flakes (optional)

Preheat the oven to 425°F. Spray a baking sheet with nonstick cooking spray.

Toss the Brussels sprouts, shallot, garlic, oil, salt, black pepper, and red pepper flakes, if using, in a large bowl.

Spread the mixture in an even layer on the prepared baking sheet.

Roast the Brussels sprouts in the oven for 15 to 20 minutes, stirring every 5 minutes, until slightly charred. Serve hot.

Tip: To add some tart sweetness to the sprouts, drizzle balsamic vinegar on top.

Tex-Mex Stuffed Bell Peppers

MAKES 4 PEPPERS

Texas-style beef and cheese meets Mexican spicy beans and peppers in this all-in-one dish. The beautiful presentation of the peppers makes your mouth water in anticipation of the delicious and satisfying filling. Once they're cooked to their warm savory goodness, I sprinkle on fresh cilantro and a squeeze of lime juice for a kick.

1 tablespoon vegetable oil

1 pound ground beef or turkey

1 garlic clove, minced

1 red onion, diced

½ teaspoon chili powder

½ teaspoon ground cumin

½ teaspoon kosher salt

½ teaspoon smoked paprika

1 green chile pepper, finely diced

1 (15-ounce) can black beans, drained and rinsed

⅓ cup water

4 variously colored large bell peppers

2 teaspoons chopped fresh cilantro, plus more for topping

2 Roma tomatoes, diced

2 cups shredded Cheddar, divided

1 lime, quartered

Preheat the oven to 350°F.

Heat the oil in a large skillet over medium-high heat until it shimmers. Add the ground beef, garlic, and red onion. Cook, stirring frequently, for 5 minutes, or until the meat, garlic, and onion are completely browned.

Immediately drain and discard the excess oil from the pan. Add the chili powder, cumin, salt, smoked paprika, green chile pepper, black beans, and water. Allow to simmer over low heat for 5 to 10 minutes.

Meanwhile, slice off the tops of the bell peppers and remove all seeds and membrane. Rinse the peppers in hot water and place upright in a 9-by-13-inch baking dish.

Spoon the meat mixture into the bell peppers until each pepper is three-quarters full. Sprinkle with cilantro and about half of the Cheddar. Cover the pan with foil and bake for 1 hour.

Remove from the oven and uncover. Add additional Cheddar and the cilantro to the top of the peppers. Let rest for 5 minutes. Squeeze lime juice over the top just before serving.

Pleasure Principle:
CARBS *for* COMFORT

It is a well-known fact that carbs are considered the world's favorite comfort food because they are warm, filling, and oh so satisfying. With my recipes for rice, pasta, and more, you are sure to please your palate and send your taste buds into orbit.

Shrimp *and* Oyster Dressing

SERVES 8 TO 10

Think homemade stuffing, but completely reimagined with soulful seafood. I even make my own corn bread. It's like the Hamptons meets downhome Memphis. No longer categorized as a side dish, this unique seafood dressing is completely hearty and absolutely filling. The aroma of the grassy green peppers, onions, and celery is unparalleled, and the lush taste of the oysters and shrimp makes a meal so good that people will be asking for more!

CORNBREAD

2 cups yellow cornmeal

¾ cup all-purpose flour

1 tablespoon granulated sugar

1½ teaspoons baking powder

½ teaspoon baking soda

¼ teaspoon kosher salt

2 large eggs, beaten

1½ cups buttermilk

6 tablespoons unsalted butter, melted

Prepare the corn bread: Preheat the oven to 425°F. Lightly grease a 9-by-13-inch baking dish.

In large bowl, mix together the cornmeal, flour, sugar, baking powder, baking soda, and salt.

In a separate bowl, mix together the beaten eggs, buttermilk, and melted butter. Stir well.

Next, pour the buttermilk mixture into the cornmeal mixture and fold together until completely wet. Pour the batter into the prepared baking dish.

Bake until the top is golden, and a toothpick comes from center of bread clean, about 20 to 25 minutes. Remove the corn bread from the oven and set aside to cool for 10 minutes.

Note: You can use already-prepared corn bread if you don't have time to bake.

Continued on page 130

DRESSING

3 tablespoons unsalted butter, plus 8 tablespoons (1 stick) melted and cooled

¼ cup chopped celery

¼ cup chopped onion

2 bell peppers, seeded and chopped (I like to use green and red)

¼ cup vegetable stock

1 teaspoon gumbo filé powder

1 teaspoon dried sage

1 teaspoon kosher salt

1 teaspoon freshly ground black pepper

¾ pound medium shrimp, peeled, deveined, and tails removed

3 cups shucked fresh oysters, drained, rinsed, and chopped into 1-inch pieces

1 (9-by-13-inch) pan corn bread (see recipe on page 128)

½ cup whole milk

2 large eggs, beaten

Prepare the dressing: Preheat the oven to 325°F. Spray a 9-by-13-inch baking dish with nonstick spray.

Melt 3 teaspoons of the butter in a large skillet over medium-high heat. Add the celery, onion, and bell peppers and sauté for 5 minutes, until vegetables are soft, stirring frequently.

Mix in the vegetable stock, gumbo filé powder, sage, salt, and pepper. Turn the heat to medium and add the shrimp and oysters to the skillet. Cook for 3 minutes, or until shrimp begins to turn pink. It doesn't need to cook all the way through. Set aside and allow to cool slightly.

In a large bowl, crumble the corn bread. Add the contents of the skillet, with milk, beaten eggs, and the 8 tablespoons of melted butter and mix thoroughly. Use your hands to mash and mix.

Transfer the seafood mixture to the baking dish. Bake, covered with foil for 20 minutes, then uncover and bake for another 15 to 20 minutes until top is golden brown and crunchy.

Let rest for 5 minutes before serving.

Creamy Cavatappi Mac & Cheese

SERVES 6 TO 8

Have a craving for creamy, homemade mac & cheese that's bursting with flavor? Then this will be your go-to recipe. It takes a little bit longer than the orange stuff in the box but trust me when I say it's worth the time and the calories, too. Hit the gym tomorrow!

8 tablespoons (1 stick) unsalted butter

½ cup all-purpose flour

1 cup whole milk

2 cups heavy cream

4 cups shredded Monterey Jack

2 cups shredded sharp white Cheddar, divided

1 tablespoon freshly grated nutmeg

1½ teaspoons kosher salt

1 teaspoon freshly ground black pepper

1 teaspoon paprika

1 pound cavatappi pasta, cooked until al dente and drained

Preheat the oven to 375°F. Spray a 9-by-13-inch casserole dish with nonstick cooking spray.

Heat a heavy-bottomed stockpot over medium-low heat. Add the butter and allow it to melt. Whisk in the flour slowly until smooth, to prevent clumps. Whisk in the milk, cream, Monterey Jack, and 1 cup of the white Cheddar. Remove from the heat. Stir in the nutmeg, salt, pepper, and paprika. Set aside.

Pour the drained pasta in an even layer into the prepared casserole dish. Cover the pasta with the cheese mixture and toss lightly to combine. Cover the dish with foil and bake for 30 minutes.

Remove the foil and sprinkle the remaining cup of white Cheddar on top. Bake for an additional 10 minutes, or until the cheese is golden brown.

Let rest for 10 minutes before serving warm.

Broccoli *and* Cheese Casserole

SERVES 6 TO 8

This recipe might remind you of the good ole days. I admit that I sometimes will use cream of mushroom soup to make a casserole that just screams comfort food to me. Don't judge! And I'm telling you that it will make a broccoli lover out of you, as well as your friends and family. It's not just a side dish, either, because tender pieces of chicken elevate this to a protein-packed meal that will leave everyone feeling healthy, happy, and satisfied.

1 (10.5-ounce) can cream of mushroom soup

½ cup whole milk

1 cup sour cream

1 cup shredded Cheddar, divided

1 pound chicken tenders, cooked and cut into small pieces (see Tip)

3 cups broccoli florets, blanched in boiling water and chopped

1 teaspoon smoked paprika

1 teaspoon cayenne pepper

1 cup cooked white rice (optional)

½ cup bread crumbs (optional)

Preheat oven to 350°F. Butter a glass 9-by-13-inch pan, or a 3-quart casserole dish.

In a large bowl, mix together the soup, milk, sour cream, and ¾ cup of Cheddar until smooth. Carefully stir in chopped chicken breast, broccoli, paprika, cayenne, and rice, if using.

Spoon the broccoli mixture into the prepared pan. Place in the oven on the middle rack. Bake, uncovered, for 30 minutes.

Remove from the oven and immediately top with the remaining Cheddar. Sprinkle bread crumbs, if using, evenly over dish. Return the dish to the oven, uncovered, and bake or broil for 10 minutes.

Remove the casserole from the oven and allow to cool for 10 minutes, and then serve.

Tip: To cook chicken, season the pieces with salt and pepper. Warm a tablespoon of vegetable or olive oil in a small frying pan on medium-high heat. Cook chicken for about 3 minutes per side, or until no longer pink inside. Let cool before cutting into small pieces.

Parmesan Meatballs *and* Spaghetti

SERVES 4 TO 6

These are not your average meatballs! They're really tender and yummy and the whole family will enjoy. The meatballs and the sauce have some of the same ingredients, so make sure you read the whole recipe before you begin. For extra cheesiness, I add a little more Parmesan on top and watch it all disappear.

1½ pounds ground beef

1 large egg

1 cup grated Parmesan, divided

¼ cup bread crumbs

1 teaspoon dried oregano, divided

1 teaspoon kosher salt, divided

1 onion, finely diced, divided

4 tablespoons olive oil, divided

2 garlic cloves, minced

4 medium tomatoes, chopped, or
    1 (15-ounce) can diced tomatoes

1 (8-ounce) can tomato sauce

2 tablespoons tomato paste

1 teaspoon dried basil

1 teaspoon granulated sugar

½ teaspoon red pepper flakes

1 pound spaghetti

Combine the beef, egg, ½ cup of the Parmesan, the bread crumbs, ½ teaspoon each of the oregano and the salt, and half of the onion in a large bowl. Use your hands to fully mix together. Proceed with hand rolling the mixture into golf ball–size spheres. Let rest.

Heat 2 tablespoons oil in a large saucepan over medium heat until shimmering. Add the remaining onion and the garlic and sauté until translucent, 5 minutes. Slowly add the tomatoes, tomato sauce, tomato paste, basil, sugar, remaining ½ teaspoon each of the oregano and the salt, and the red pepper flakes. Cover and simmer for 10 to 20 minutes. Remove from the heat.

While the sauce is cooking, heat the remaining 2 tablespoons of oil in large skillet over medium-high heat until shimmering. Fry the meatballs for 3 to 4 minutes per side, longer if necessary, until they are firm to the touch. Work in batches, if needed. Set aside to drain on paper towels, or, if you wish, add to the sauce.

Prepare spaghetti according to package directions. Drain.

Serve spaghetti with the sauce and meatballs. Garnish with the remaining ½ cup of grated Parmesan.

Tip: If you are short on time, you can replace the homemade sauce with store-bought. Sprinkle the finished dish with chopped fresh parsley for a lovely presentation.

Lobster Mac & Cheese

SERVES 4 TO 6

Mac & cheese is a soulful side dish that folks I know take very seriously. To make it more fabulous, I add a nice helping of lobster. The bubbling-hot cheesy sauce, melting over the pasta, studded with lobster . . . my, my, my, this is good eating at its finest. It will have everyone singing your name like Beyoncé!

1 (1-pound) lobster, or 4 ounces cooked lobster meat

3 tablespoons unsalted butter

3 tablespoons all-purpose flour

2 cups whole milk

1 cup shredded smoked Gouda

1 cup shredded Gruyère, divided

½ cup shredded Cheddar

1 teaspoon freshly ground white pepper

1 teaspoon dry mustard

½ teaspoon garlic powder

½ teaspoon onion powder

1 teaspoon kosher salt, or more to taste

¼ cup bread crumbs (optional)

½ pound elbow macaroni, cooked until al dente and drained

Truffle oil, to serve

If using fresh lobster, see tip for how to prepare. If using pre-cooked lobster meat, cut it into bite-size pieces.

Preheat the oven to 350°F.

Heat a heavy-bottomed stockpot over medium-low heat. Add the butter and allow it to melt. Whisk in the flour slowly until smooth, to prevent clumps, and cook until lightly browned. Whisk in the milk, Gouda, ½ cup Gruyère, and Cheddar until smooth. Remove from the heat. Stir in the pepper, mustard, garlic powder, onion powder, and salt.

Stir the cooked macaroni and lobster meat into the cheese mixture.

Spray a 1½-quart casserole dish with nonstick cooking spray. Transfer the lobster mixture to the prepared casserole. Top with remaining ½ cup Gruyère and bread crumbs, if using. Bake for 10 to 20 minutes, uncovered, until the cheese is bubbling. Remove from the oven and allow to cool for 10 minutes before serving.

Plate servings in shallow bowls. Drizzle with the truffle oil.

Tip: To cook fresh lobster: Bring 2 quarts of water and 1 teaspoon of salt to a boil in a large stockpot. Plunge the lobster headfirst into the pot. It should be fully submerged. Cover tightly and bring the water to a boil again. Lower the heat to medium-high and cook for 10 to 15 minutes, until bright red. Using tongs, remove the lobster from the water and allow it to cool on a bed of ice. Next, crack the lobster and remove all the meat from the tail and claw cavities. Cut the meat into pieces.

Parmesan Rosemary Scalloped Potatoes

SERVES 6 TO 8

Sometimes a plain ole potato just won't do as a side dish; however, when you add a little cheese and aromatic herbs, you turn bland potatoes into a dish percolating with flavor. Pair with your favorite meat, especially beef, such as the Red Wine Braised Pot Roast (page 177), and get ready to be thrilled.

3 tablespoons unsalted butter

¼ cup all-purpose flour

2 cups whole milk

½ cup heavy cream

2 teaspoons minced garlic

1 teaspoon dried rosemary

1 teaspoon kosher salt

½ teaspoon freshly ground black pepper

½ teaspoon paprika

3 pounds Yukon Gold potatoes, peeled and sliced ⅛ inch thick

¾ cup grated Parmesan

¼ cup shredded mozzarella

Preheat the oven to 350°F.

Brown 2 tablespoons of the butter in a large saucepan over medium-high heat. Once the foam subsides, stir in the flour until creamy. Lower the heat and cook about 3 minutes, stirring constantly, until roux is golden brown.

Slowly pour in the milk, stirring to prevent lumps. Increase the heat to medium-high, and add the cream. Cook, stirring frequently, for 5 minutes. Remove the saucepan from the heat, and add the remaining tablespoon of butter and the garlic, rosemary, salt, pepper, and paprika. Stir well, then fully submerge sliced potatoes into the creamy mixture.

Transfer the creamy potato mixture to a lidded 9-by-13-inch cast-iron baking dish. Add ½ cup of the Parmesan and all of the mozzarella. Cover and bake for 40 minutes.

Remove from the oven and remove the lid. Sprinkle the remaining ¼ cup of the Parmesan over the top and return the dish, uncovered, to the oven. Bake for an additional 10 minutes.

Herb-Roasted Bliss Potatoes

SERVES 6 TO 8

These delicious and crispy potatoes are an excellent side dish that can be served with dinner or breakfast. It's completely simple to make, and once you add that olive oil and oregano, not only is the aroma divine, so is the taste! This side pairs perfectly with Sun-Dried Tomato Cornish Hens (page 197).

3 pounds baby potatoes, whole, or small red potatoes, quartered

¼ cup olive oil

4 tablespoons (½ stick) unsalted butter, melted

3 garlic cloves, minced

2 tablespoons minced fresh parsley

1 teaspoon dried oregano

2 teaspoons kosher salt

1 teaspoon freshly ground black pepper

Preheat the oven to 400°F.

Combine the potatoes, oil, and butter in a large bowl and stir the potatoes to evenly coat. Add the garlic, parsley, oregano, salt, and pepper and stir well to ensure that the seasonings evenly coat each piece of potato.

Spray a medium roasting pan with light coat of nonstick cooking spray. Transfer the potatoes to the pan and spread evenly. Roast, uncovered, for 25 minutes. The potatoes should be crisp and golden.

Remove from the pan and serve.

Sweet Potato Soufflé
with Orange Zest *and* Caramelized Sugar

SERVES 6 TO 8

This is a very light and airy sweet potato casserole. The combination of allspice, brown sugar, and orange zest helps lift the flavors of the potatoes, making this side dish almost like eating dessert with your dinner. Pair this dish with a heavy protein such as the Beef Short Ribs (page 173) and your belly will truly be satisfied.

5 medium sweet potatoes, peeled, boiled, and drained

8 tablespoons (1 stick) unsalted butter, at room temperature

2 large eggs, beaten

1 cup granulated sugar

2 teaspoons vanilla extract

Zest and juice of 1 orange

Juice of 1 lemon

⅓ cup whole milk

1 teaspoon ground allspice

1 teaspoon kosher salt

3 tablespoons brown sugar

Preheat the oven to 350°F. Spray a 9-by-13-inch casserole dish with nonstick cooking spray.

Combine the sweet potatoes, butter, and eggs in a large bowl and use an electric mixer to mix on low speed.

One at a time, slowly add the sugar, vanilla, orange juice and zest, lemon juice, milk, allspice, and salt, mixing until completely combined.

Pour the sweet potato mixture into the prepared casserole dish and spread out evenly. Sprinkle the top lightly with the brown sugar. Bake for 40 minutes, or until the top begins to caramelize.

Remove from the oven and allow to rest for 5 minutes before serving warm.

Creole Rice Pilaf

SERVES 4 TO 6

The vibrant yellow rice in this pilaf makes it more than just a simple side dish. I use lots of aromatics such as ginger, onion, scallions, and, of course, red pepper flakes, so I promise you that it tastes as good as it looks. This will pair perfectly with any of the meats in this book. You can try it with fish, too, to switch it up.

2 tablespoons vegetable oil

¼ teaspoon red pepper flakes

1 celery rib, chopped

1 yellow onion, diced

½ cup chopped scallions

1 (8-ounce) bag yellow rice mix

3 cups chicken stock

2 Roma tomatoes, diced

1 teaspoon dried thyme

1 tablespoon roughly chopped fresh parsley

1 teaspoon kosher salt

¼ teaspoon freshly ground black pepper

¼ teaspoon cayenne pepper

Heat the oil in a medium saucepan over medium-high heat. Add the red pepper flakes, celery, onion, and scallions. Sauté for 5 minutes. Add the yellow rice mix and chicken stock and bring to a boil. Cook for 3 minutes, stirring frequently.

Slowly add the tomatoes, thyme, parsley, salt, black pepper, and cayenne. Cover and lower the heat to low. Simmer for 45 minutes.

Remove from the heat and allow to rest for 5 minutes. Fluff with a fork, and serve.

Coconut Rice *and* Peas

SERVES 6 TO 8

I love the Caribbean—especially the food! This combination of coconut with rice and "peas"—kidney beans to you and me—is always a flashback to good meals I've enjoyed during my travels. Both the beans and the rice are cooked directly in coconut milk and then the finished dish is sprinkled with buttery toasted coconut to give it that authentic island flavor. Simply amazing!

2 cups dried kidney beans, picked over and soaked overnight

2 tablespoons unsalted butter

1 large shallot, minced

2 garlic cloves, minced

1 tablespoon minced oregano

1 sprig thyme

2 (14-ounce) cans unsweetened coconut milk

2 cups long-grained white rice

1 tablespoon kosher salt

1½ teaspoons freshly ground black pepper

1 cup toasted shredded coconut, for garnish

Chopped scallions, for garnish (optional)

In a medium stock pot, bring 4 quarts of water to a boil. Add beans and stir. Cover pot and reduce heat to low. Allow beans to simmer for 1 hour. Remove from heat.

Drain beans and rinse out stock pot.

In clean pot, melt butter over medium-high heat. Add shallot, garlic, oregano, and thyme. Sauté for about 5 minutes. Add to the beans to the pot.

Add coconut milk, rice, salt, and pepper and stir to combine. Bring to a boil, then reduce heat to low. Cover and simmer covered for 12 to 15 minutes, or until rice is cooked through.

Remove from heat and let rest 5 to 10 minutes, covered. Fluff with fork before serving and garnish with shredded toasted coconut and chopped scallions, if using.

Tip: For a faster dish, use three 16-ounce cans of kidney beans. Rinse and add after the rice has cooked.

Succulent
SEAFOOD *Sensations*

Don't get me started about my love for seafood, it's what makes me happiest to cook or eat. So when I say I put my heart and soul into these recipes, you better believe it. If you're anything like me, as a seafood lover, you will enjoy creating these succulent main dishes from the treasures of the sea: fish, shrimp, scallops, and more! You might notice that the fish recipes are designed for two. These are recipes that need attention, so I usually make these for someone special, not for a larger crowd.

Shrimp *in* White Wine Butter Sauce

SERVES 4

This is one of my favorite go-to meals, as it comes together in about 20 minutes and is great for company or a casual weeknight dinner. I use both butter and olive oil in this sauce and the combination makes it rich enough to cling really well to rice, pasta, or whatever you serve it with. Make sure to use good-quality wine and save some for drinking!

3 tablespoons olive oil

4 tablespoons (½ stick) unsalted butter

4 garlic cloves, minced

½ cup dry white wine

⅓ cup chicken stock

1 tablespoon capers

½ teaspoon paprika

½ teaspoon freshly ground black pepper

2 pounds extra-large shrimp, peeled and deveined

Zest and juice of 2 lemons

¼ teaspoon red pepper flakes (optional)

⅓ cup chopped fresh parsley

Cooked pasta or rice, for serving

Melt the butter and olive oil in a large skillet. Add the garlic and sauté for 1 minute. Add the wine, stock, capers, paprika, and black pepper. Bring to a simmer and allow to reduce, 3 to 5 minutes.

Add the shrimp to the sauce and sauté until pink and opaque, about 4 minutes.

Remove from the heat and top with the lemon zest and juice, red pepper flakes, if using, and the parsley.

Serve over pasta or rice.

Tip: Thinly slice a lemon into rounds and toss into the pasta for presentation.

Blackened Sea Scallops

SERVES 2

Scallops are a real treat. I like to make them when someone special is coming by or even sometimes for myself. I'm very busy and when a good meal is in order, these exceptional blackened scallops are an excellent choice. They're not burned black, it's the Cajun rub that creates the look. It infuses the scallops with the flavors of the Gulf Coast. Pair them with a nice glass of chardonnay and my Sautéed Lemon-Garlic Asparagus (page 109). You can thank me later!

CAJUN RUB

1 teaspoon kosher salt

1 teaspoon red pepper flakes

⅛ teaspoon cayenne pepper

1 teaspoon garlic powder

1 teaspoon paprika

½ teaspoon freshly grated nutmeg

SCALLOPS

1 pound large fresh sea scallops

1 tablespoon olive oil

2 tablespoons unsalted butter, at room temperature

Juice of 1 lemon

Prepare the rub: Stir together the salt, red pepper flakes, cayenne, garlic powder, paprika, and nutmeg in a shallow bowl. Set aside.

Prepare the scallops: Pat each scallop dry with a paper towel and then dredge on all sides in the spice mixture, shaking off any excess (they should be well-coated).

Heat oil in a large cast iron skillet over high heat until almost smoking.

Place scallops into the skillet and do not move. Allow the scallops to cook on the first side for 2 to 3 minutes until they form a golden crust and are easy to flip. Flip, add the butter, and allow to sear for another 2 to 3 minutes on the other side. Using a large spoon, baste the scallops with the melted butter throughout the process. Remove from the pan, drizzle with additional butter sauce from the bottom of the pan and lemon juice. Serve immediately.

Note: It's easy to double or triple this recipe if you want. Just make more rub and use more scallops. Depending on the size of your skillet, you may not need more butter or olive oil for coating and cooking, but, if needed, more butter never hurt anyone!

Set realistic expectations for yourself.

I caution you to not to get too far ahead of yourself and overestimate your newly developed skills. It is always better to undersell and overdeliver. I know it is easy to get excited after you prepare a great meal, especially when you really want to impress someone, but you don't want to find yourself in a real-life pop-quiz situation because you told your man you could cook all of his favorite meals. You'll end up like my girl Nicole, calling me from her date's kitchen in a panic, trying to figure out how to make branzino. You see, she slightly embellished her cooking abilities on their first date, when her chicken lettuce wraps turned out so well. She began to say that she could make any and every dish that came to mind, despite most of those dishes being uncharted territory for her.

Unbeknownst to her, for their fifth date, her guy planned a romantic evening that included her making branzino. She spent 30 minutes in the bathroom on the phone with me and on Google, trying to hide the fact that she had never even tasted it, let alone tried to cook it! After hanging up with me, she came up with a plan: she followed the first couple of steps that she could remember from the recipe, and then "accidentally" dropped the fish on the floor. She ended up throwing in the hat and ordered in.

Seared Branzino *with* Fennel *and* Lemon Caper Sauce

SERVES 2

Do you love eating branzino when you're out at a nice restaurant? Well, I'm bringing the restaurant to your kitchen table with this recipe. This mild white fish is stuffed with fresh rosemary, fennel, and thin slices of lemon, and it makes a dramatic presentation on the plate. Don't worry about the capers being too salty; the citrus from the lemon smoothes out the salt, making them a perfect match for your palate.

1 whole branzino, gutted

4 rosemary sprigs

1 head fennel, fronds removed and diced

2 garlic cloves, minced

2 lemons, cut into wedges

2 teaspoons kosher salt

1 teaspoon freshly ground black pepper

2 tablespoons olive oil

½ cup mixed olives, halved (optional)

4 slices onion, halved (optional)

LEMON CAPER SAUCE

2 tablespoons unsalted butter

2 garlic cloves, minced

½ cup stock (see Note)

Juice of 2 lemons

3 tablespoons capers

1 tablespoon dried parsley

1 teaspoon kosher salt

Preheat the oven to 400°F.

Rinse the branzino in cold water and pat dry.

Stuff the stomach cavity of the whole fish with the rosemary, fennel, half of the minced garlic, and half of a lemon's worth of wedges. Season both sides of the fish with the salt, pepper, and the remaining garlic. Rub the seasoning into the skin.

Heat the oil in a large, ovenproof skillet over medium-high heat. Transfer the fish to the center of the skillet. Sear each side for 4 minutes per side. Make sure there is a golden crisp beginning to form on each side, then flip. Top with olives and onion slices, if using.

Transfer the skillet to the oven and bake, uncovered, for 10 minutes. Remove from the oven and set aside.

Prepare the sauce: In small saucepan, melt the butter in a small saucepan over medium heat. Add the garlic and cook until browned and crisp.

Add the stock and bring to a boil. Allow the stock to reduce by half. Lower the heat and add the lemon juice, capers, parsley, and salt. Allow the sauce to simmer and thicken 2 minutes.

Remove from the heat and transfer to a sauce dish. Drizzle sauce over the fish and serve with extra sauce on the side.

Note: If you have seafood stock, use it here, otherwise vegetable stock or even white wine will work.

Cornmeal-Dusted Catfish

SERVES 2

This buttery, hearty, oh-so Southern dish will make your soul happy, baby. I like it crispy and served with hot sauce—the spicier, the better. This fish is very versatile and can be perfectly paired with some Creamy Cavatappi Mac & Cheese (page 133) and Southern Turnip Greens (page 110) or placed between two slices of bread with a little coleslaw to make a good ole catfish sandwich.

1 cup vegetable oil

1 cup yellow cornmeal

1 tablespoon seasoning salt

1 tablespoon paprika

½ teaspoon ground turmeric

½ teaspoon cayenne pepper

1 teaspoon ground cumin

1 teaspoon kosher salt

Freshly ground black pepper

2 whole catfish fillets

1 lemon, cut into wedges, for garnish

Pour the oil into a large cast-iron skillet and heat over medium-high heat.

Combine the cornmeal, seasoning salt, paprika, turmeric, cayenne, cumin, salt, and pinch of pepper in a bowl. Dredge the fish with cornmeal mixture, coating well on both sides.

Transfer the fish, skin side up, to the skillet. Cook for 6 to 8 minutes on each side, creating a golden brown crust.

Remove from the oil and drain on a wire rack. Sprinkle with another pinch of pepper, transfer to a serving dish, and garnish with the lemon.

Pecan-Crusted Trout

SERVES 2

Quiet as this secret is kept, the combination of fish and nuts is an absolutely delightful match. Pecans are a Southern favorite, and with their buttery crunch, they taste great with the delicate trout—some say that trout itself has a buttery taste. It's everything you can expect from a freshwater fish and is simply delectable! I add a surprising zing of nutmeg to make this recipe one to remember.

1 teaspoon kosher salt

½ teaspoon freshly ground black
   pepper

⅓ cup ground pecans

2 tablespoons chopped fresh parsley

½ cup panko bread crumbs

¼ cup vegetable oil

2 fresh skin-on trout fillets

2 tablespoons unsalted butter

¼ teaspoon freshly grated nutmeg

½ cup radish sprouts

1 lemon, sliced into wedges, for garnish

Mix together the salt, pepper, pecans, parsley, and the bread crumbs in a shallow bowl.

Pour the oil into a large skillet and bring to a simmer over medium heat.

Skinless side up, coat the trout with the pecan mixture. Transfer the trout, coated side down, to the skillet. Cook for 2 to 3 minutes, then flip and cook for an additional 3 minutes, or until the fish has achieved an opaque center.

Meanwhile, melt the butter in a small saucepan over medium heat and add the nutmeg.

Arrange the radish sprouts into a bed on a serving plate and place the baked trout on top. Drizzle with the melted butter mixture and garnish with lemon wedges.

Baked Strawberry Grouper

SERVES 2

There are no strawberries in this recipe, so don't be fooled! This fish is so damn good. It is a light, mild-flavored fish that pairs wonderfully with these vegetables. The okra and greens balance the sweetness of the fish and the Creole seasoning gives it the essence of the islands. A few tablespoons of Fish Tea Soup Mix gives this a Jamaican flair.

2 (8-ounce) Strawberry Grouper fillets, cleaned and trimmed

1 teaspoon kosher salt, plus more for seasoning vegetables

1 teaspoon freshly ground black pepper, plus more for seasoning vegetables

1 teaspoon Creole seasoning, plus more for seasoning vegetables

1 small yellow onion, sliced

1 habanero pepper, seeded and thinly sliced

1 cup sliced, fresh okra

1 small kabocha squash, peeled and diced

2 to 3 heads baby bok choy, trimmed, rinsed, and sliced

½ teaspoon cayenne pepper

½ cup seafood stock

2 tablespoons Fish Tea Soup Mix (optional; see Note)

1 tablespoon unsalted butter, cold

Preheat the oven to 350°F.

Rinse the grouper with cold water and pat dry. Season with the salt, pepper, and Creole seasoning on both sides of the fish. Set aside.

In a glass baking dish large enough to fit both fillets easily, toss the onion, pepper, okra, squash, and bok choy with the salt, pepper, seasoning, and cayenne pepper. Add stock and toss again.

Cover the dish and cook about 10 minutes to soften the vegetables. Remove from oven, and carefully uncover.

Nestle the grouper fillets into the vegetables. Sprinkle with Fish Tea Soup Mix. Slice the butter into small pieces and sprinkle them evenly over the vegetables and fish.

Cover the dish again and return to the oven for 10 minutes or until the fish begins to flake.

Orange-Ginger Glazed Salmon

SERVES 2

If you're as busy as I am, you need this recipe: it's easy and fast. The sweetness from the orange and aromatic scent lightens up the salmon, and the ginger heightens the flavor. This meal is perfectly complemented by brown or white rice. This is a great dish for beginners as you don't have to worry too much about overcooking the salmon, and the sauce is to die for!

1 pound skin-on salmon fillets

1 teaspoon kosher salt

1 teaspoon freshly ground black pepper

Juice of 2 oranges

5 tablespoons honey

1 teaspoon minced fresh ginger

2 garlic cloves, minced

1 teaspoon sesame oil

2 teaspoons soy sauce

2 tablespoons olive oil

1 scallion, trimmed and chopped, for garnish

Cooked basmati rice or whole-grain pasta, for serving

Season the salmon on both sides with the salt and pepper. Set aside.

Whisk together the orange juice, honey, ginger, garlic, sesame oil, and soy sauce in a small bowl. Set aside.

Heat the olive oil in a medium skillet over medium-high heat. Place the salmon in the center of the pan and cook on each side for 3 minutes until it releases easily from the pan.

Lower the heat and coat the salmon with the sauce. Allow the sauce to marry with the salmon for 2 minutes.

Transfer the salmon to a serving dish and garnish with the scallions. Serve with basmati rice or whole-grain pasta.

Red Snapper Escovitch

SERVES 2

I love to travel to the Caribbean, not only for the relaxing tropical breeze and amazing sights, but also for the food! This is one of my signature dishes, perfect to cook for a date night. It's a brilliant dish: the colorful garnish of bell peppers and the distinct flavors of garlic, ginger, and citrus bring the islands right into your kitchen. Serve it with my Coconut Rice and Peas (page 147).

ESCOVITCH

1 sweet yellow onion, halved and thinly sliced

1 Scotch bonnet pepper, stemmed, seeded, and thinly sliced

3 bell peppers, seeded and thinly sliced (I use green, yellow, and red)

1 sprig thyme

1 tablespoon chopped fresh cilantro

1 teaspoon whole black peppercorns

2 cloves garlic, minced

½ cup white vinegar

1 teaspoon olive oil

1 teaspoon kosher salt

SNAPPER

1 (2-pound) whole red snapper, scaled and gutted

1 tablespoon Cajun seasoning

1 teaspoon kosher salt

½ teaspoon cayenne pepper

2 cups canola oil

2 cups fish fry crumbs (such as McCormick's)

1 lemon, sliced

1 lime, sliced

Prepare the Escovitch (at least 1 day before you plan to cook the snapper): In a large mixing bowl, add the onion, peppers, thyme, cilantro, peppercorns, garlic, white vinegar, olive oil, and salt.

Toss well to combine, transfer to a large pickling or mason jar, and refrigerate for at least 1 day or up to 3 days, shaking the jar every now and then (make sure the lid is on tight).

Prepare the snapper: Rinse the snapper in cold water and place on a baking sheet to season.

Combine the Cajun seasoning, salt, and cayenne in a small bowl. Season the fish liberally with this mix. Set aside.

In a frying pan large enough to accommodate the snapper from head to tail, add the canola oil and heat over medium-high heat.

Spread the fish fry crumbs on a plate, and fully coat the seasoned snapper with the crumbs, patting them with your hands to stick firmly. You will have fish fry crumbs left over but you need enough to be able to coat the fish fully.

Test the oil by adding a few crumbs from the fish fry—it should sizzle gently in the oil. If it sinks to the bottom, the oil isn't hot enough.

When the oil is hot, add the red snapper. Cook for 5 to 10 minutes, or until fish releases easily from the pan. Carefully flip fish over and cook another 5 to 10 minutes or until the coating is crispy and the fish flakes easily.

Remove the snapper to a plate lined with paper towels to absorb excess oil. Once it has drained, place on a serving dish.

Squeeze lemon and lime juice over fish, top with the prepared Escovitch sauce, and serve.

Pot Rattlers: FOOD that SATISFIES the SOUL

Being Southern grown, we eat food that sticks to our bones. We like meats that hold flavor, fill our belly, and stick to our hips in all the right places. Everything we eat is homemade, so get ready—there will be pots rattling in your kitchen because my recipes require you to throw down!

Brown Stewed Chicken

SERVES 6 TO 8

This may not be the most beautiful dish, but best believe the taste will blow you away. This Jamaican classic, one of my favorites, is a hearty stew perfect for Netflix-and-chill evenings. The Scotch bonnet pepper will keep you warm inside, especially when it is chilly outside. Not only does this stew taste delish, but it's also very good for you with its medley of vegetables and fresh-cut chicken. Trust me, one bowl will comfort you for an entire evening. Use a large saucepan or Dutch oven with a lid for this recipe—it must fit all the chicken.

CHICKEN

4 pounds fresh skin-on chicken parts (legs, thighs, breasts cut in half, wings)

1 cup white vinegar

Juice of 2 limes

3 tablespoons kosher salt

MARINADE

2 large tomatoes, chopped

2 sweet yellow onions, chopped

2 Scotch bonnet peppers, chopped (see Note)

4 garlic cloves, minced

6 scallions, chopped

2 teaspoons ground allspice

2 teaspoons kosher salt

4 thyme sprigs

¼ cup vegetable oil

Prepare the chicken: Place the chicken in a large bowl in your sink. Pour the vinegar and lime juice over chicken and sprinkle with salt. Rub the mixture over the chicken. Add cold water to the bowl from the faucet until nearly full and thoroughly rinse the chicken in the mixture. Run water over the chicken as you lift it up and out of the bowl. Empty and rinse the bowl and return the chicken to the empty bowl.

Prepare the marinade: Mix all of the ingredients for the marinade together in a large bowl, except for the vegetable oil and the thyme. Divide the marinade ingredients in half. Place one half of the marinade ingredients in the bowl with the chicken and add the oil and the thyme. Set the second half of the marinade ingredients aside. Toss to completely coat the chicken in the marinade, cover and allow to sit at room temperature for 20 minutes.

Continued on page 172

STEW

1 tablespoon vegetable oil

1 carrot, peeled and thinly sliced

1 teaspoon kosher salt

¼ teaspoon freshly ground black
pepper

1 tablespoon all-purpose flour

3 cups chicken stock

¼ cup ketchup

3 tablespoons tomato paste

2 tablespoons browning seasoning

1 habanero pepper, thinly sliced (see
Note)

4 thyme sprigs

2 (15-ounce) cans butter beans, drained
and rinsed

Cooked rice or steamed cabbage, for
serving

Prepare the stew: Heat the oil in a large saucepan or Dutch oven over medium-high heat. Line a plate with paper towels and remove chicken pieces from the marinade. Working in batches, brown each piece of chicken on both sides about 4 to 5 minutes per side, discarding the marinade. Remove the browned chicken from the pot and transfer to a paper towel to drain any excess oil.

Add the reserved marinade and the carrots and cook until softened and lightly browned, about 5 minutes. Season with salt and pepper. Add up to 2 tablespoons more oil if they are sticking.

Sprinkle with the flour and cook 2 to 3 minutes. Slowly whisk in chicken stock, scraping the browned bits up from the bottom of the pan. Stir in the ketchup, tomato paste, and browning seasoning. Bring to a rolling boil, stirring to keep vegetables from sticking.

Nestle chicken back into the pot with the habanero pepper and the thyme. Cover the pot. Reduce the heat to low and allow to simmer for about 30 minutes, or until chicken is cooked through and reaches 165°F on a meat thermometer. Add the butter beans during the last 10 minutes of cooking.

Remove from the heat, discard the thyme sprigs, and serve with rice or steamed cabbage.

Note: I like my food spicy so I leave in the pepper seeds, but if you want to reduce the heat, seed the peppers before cutting them. Make sure to wear gloves and don't touch your eyes after as those seeds are hot.

Beef Short Ribs

SERVES 4 TO 6

Beef short ribs are pretty much foolproof and you're in for some good eating as long as two things come together. First, the beef must be impeccably braised—I'm talking crispy, caramelized, and browned to perfection. Second, make sure that the ribs are tender to the bone, and just like that, they're done. Stick a fork in them and enjoy!

1 teaspoon kosher salt

1 teaspoon freshly ground black pepper

1 teaspoon freshly grated nutmeg

1 teaspoon paprika

4 pounds bone-in short ribs

¼ cup olive oil

1 small onion, chopped

2 garlic cloves, minced

4 cups beef stock

2 tablespoons Worcestershire sauce

1 rosemary sprig

1 thyme sprig

1 tablespoon Dijon mustard

Preheat the oven to 375°F.

Combine the salt, pepper, nutmeg, and paprika in a small bowl. Fully coat the ribs with this seasoning mixture.

Heat 2 tablespoons of the oil in a large, ovenproof Dutch oven or heavy-bottomed pot with a lid over medium-high heat, until the oil is shimmering. Sear the ribs for 2 to 3 minutes per side and in batches, if necessary. Add more oil as needed. Remove to a plate and set aside.

In same pot, combine the onion and garlic and sauté for 3 minutes. Add the beef stock and Worcestershire sauce, scraping the browned bits up from the bottom of the pot. Bring to a boil then reduce to a simmer. Add the ribs back to the pot, making sure they aren't completely submerged in the liquid. Place the rosemary and thyme sprigs atop the ribs. Cover and place in in the oven. Bake for 2 to 2½ hours or until the meat is falling from the bones.

Remove from the oven, stir the mustard into the broth mixture, and serve warm with the broth from the skillet.

Memphis Soul Stew

SERVES 8

My hometown of Memphis really loves a meal that sticks to your bones, and my Memphis stew does just that. It's very tasty, like a gumbo with sirloin instead of seafood. I like to think of it as a Cajun chili. It's not a typical beef stew either. I add chicken along with the steak. Add potatoes, carrots, and tomatoes, and this stew becomes more exciting with each bite.

4 tablespoons (½ stick) unsalted butter, divided

2 pounds skin-on chicken leg quarters

2 teaspoons kosher salt, divided

2 teaspoons red pepper flakes, divided

1 pound ground sirloin steak

1 yellow onion, chopped

1 green bell pepper, seeded and chopped

2 carrots, peeled and diced

2 garlic cloves, chopped

1 teaspoon freshly ground black pepper

1 (6-ounce) can tomato paste

4 tablespoons all-purpose flour

4 cups beef stock

1 cup water

3 large tomatoes, chopped

2 Idaho potatoes, skin on and chopped

Melt 2 tablespoons of the butter in a large heavy-bottomed pot or Dutch oven over medium-high heat. Pat the chicken quarters dry with paper towels and season with 1 teaspoon salt. Add the chicken to the pan and season with ½ teaspoon red pepper flakes. Brown on each side, 6 minutes per side, flipping frequently to prevent burning.

Remove the chicken from the pan and roughly chop the meat from the bone, discarding the skin. Set aside.

Melt 1 tablespoon of butter in the same pan. Add the ground sirloin and brown, stirring frequently, for 4 minutes. Season with ½ teaspoon salt. Drain excess liquid.

Move the beef to one side of the pan and add the remaining 1 tablespoon of butter. Add the onion, bell pepper, carrots, and garlic and cook for another 4 minutes, until softened. Season with remaining salt, red pepper flakes, and pepper. Add the tomato paste and allow to cook for 1 minute until lightly caramelized, then mix into the beef and vegetable mixture. Add the flour and stir to coat the beef mixture. Allow to cook for another minute. Add the beef stock and water, scraping the browned bits up from the bottom of the pan. Bring to a boil then reduce to a simmer and add the chopped chicken, tomatoes, and potatoes.

Partially cover the pot and allow to simmer for 30 to 45 minutes, stirring occasionally to prevent the bottom from burning, until the vegetables and potatoes are tender. If the stew is too thick, add additional water. Remove from the heat and serve hot.

Red Wine Braised Pot Roast

SERVES 6

Break out your grown-up palate because this meal is for the grown and sexy, with red wine that adds a bold and luscious taste. Instead of the standard onion soup and mushroom treatment, I added garlic, thyme, rosemary, and a bay leaf that makes the meat the star of the show. I find that green beans and carrots are the perfect co-stars and will leave you wanting an encore.

1 (4-pound) chuck shoulder roast, trimmed

1 tablespoon kosher salt, divided

1½ teaspoons freshly ground black pepper

2 tablespoons olive oil

2 white onions, diced large

2 garlic cloves, chopped

2 thyme sprigs

2 rosemary sprigs

1 bay leaf

1 cup dry red wine, such as cabernet sauvignon, merlot, or pinot noir

4 cups beef stock

3 carrots, peeled and chopped

Preheat the oven to 375°F.

Season the roast evenly with 1½ teaspoons each of the salt and pepper. Heat oil in large Dutch oven or heavy bottomed-pot over medium-high heat. Brown roast on all sides, 6 to 10 minutes. Remove the roast from the pot.

To the same pot add the white onions and sauté until translucent, about 5 to 6 minutes.

Add the garlic, thyme, rosemary, and bay leaf and cook for 1 to 2 minutes. Season with remaining salt. Deglaze the pan with ¾ cup wine, scraping the browned bits up from the bottom of the pot. Allow the wine to reduce by half. Add the beef stock, bring to a boil then add the chuck roast back to the pan.

Cover the Dutch oven and bake for 1 hour. At the 1-hour mark, add the remaining ¼ cup of wine and the carrots. Roast for an additional 1 to 1½ hours, or until the vegetables are done. Slice or shred to serve.

Stewed Oxtails

SERVES 2 TO 4

This is one Jamaican dish that I can't get enough of, although eating it at your favorite Jamaican restaurant can be expensive. Why not try making it at home? This robust stew has a savory gravy created using onion, garlic, allspice, smoked paprika, and thyme sprigs that give it a very delectable island flavor. Once you try making this dish at home, you'll want to make it over and over again.

2 pounds large oxtails, cut into pieces

2 tablespoons vegetable oil

Kosher salt

Freshly ground black pepper

Smoked paprika

½ teaspoon cayenne pepper

1 sweet Vidalia onion, chopped

2 garlic cloves, minced

1 teaspoon minced fresh ginger

1 tablespoon ground allspice

1 teaspoon curry powder

½ cup chopped scallions

2 thyme sprigs

2 tablespoons browning seasoning

3 tablespoons all-purpose flour

6 cups beef stock

1 tablespoon Worcestershire sauce

3 tablespoons tomato paste

1 tomato, chopped

1 Scotch bonnet pepper, chopped

Juice of 1 lime

Cooked rice and peas, for serving

Thoroughly rinse the oxtails under cool water. Pat dry with paper towels and set aside.

Heat the oil in a stockpot or Dutch oven over high heat until shimmering. Add the oxtails and season with ½ teaspoon each of the salt, black pepper, smoked paprika, and cayenne. Cook, stirring frequently, to evenly brown the oxtails.

Lower the heat to medium and stir in the onion, garlic, ginger, allspice, curry powder, ½ teaspoon smoked paprika, half of the scallions, the thyme, and 1 tablespoon of the browning seasoning. Cook until fragrant, about 5 minutes. Sprinkle with the flour and stir, coating the meat in the flour and browning it.

Slowly pour in the beef stock, stirring to keep the meat from sticking to the pan. Add the remaining tablespoon of browning seasoning, the Worcestershire sauce, tomato paste, tomato, Scotch bonnet pepper, and lime juice. Stir to combine and add the remaining scallions. Bring to a boil.

Lower the heat and cover. Allow the stew to simmer, covered, for 2 hours, stirring frequently. Remove from the heat, discard thyme sprigs, and season with salt and black pepper to taste. Serve with rice and peas or cabbage.

Tip: This dish can also be made with butter beans and potatoes. Add a can of drained beans or 1 cup of chopped potato (about 1 potato) with the broth.

Turkey Necks *in* Vidalia Gravy

SERVES 4 TO 6

When I am in the mood for a warm and wholesome meal, I turn to this hearty dish. Not only is it a savory Southern favorite, but it is also packed with loads of flavor that leaves you feeling satisfied. Personally, I like to serve it over rice and add a little kick with hot sauce. Trust me, this is a meal that keeps on giving!

6 fresh turkey necks (about 4 pounds)

2 tablespoons kosher salt

1 teaspoon freshly ground black pepper

1 teaspoon seasoning salt

½ teaspoon red pepper flakes

Juice of 1 lemon

¼ cup vegetable oil

VIDALIA GRAVY

4 sweet Vidalia onions, thinly sliced

4 celery ribs, diced

4 garlic cloves, chopped

4 tablespoons all-purpose flour

4 cups vegetable stock

½ cup chopped scallions

Cooked rice or mashed potatoes, for serving

Preheat the oven to 400°F.

Season the turkey necks with the salt, black pepper, seasoning salt, red pepper flakes, and lemon juice.

Heat the oil in a large saucepan over medium-high heat. Add the seasoned turkey necks and brown on all sides, about 5 minutes. Transfer to a large roasting pan and set aside.

Make the gravy: In the same pan, stirring constantly, sauté the onions and celery over medium heat until liquid is released and vegetables are very soft, about 10 minutes. Turn up heat to medium-high, and add garlic. Saute for another 2 to 3 minutes until browned.

Sprinkle the flour over the vegetables and stir until the veggies are completely covered with the flour. Slowly pour in the stock and, stirring continuously, bring to a simmer to thicken. If you can't fit all the stock into the pan, pour the excess stock into the roasting pot. It is going into the oven and will come together there.

Pour the gravy over the turkey necks (and any additional stock) in the roasting pan, along with the scallions. Cover and place in the oven on the middle rack. Roast for 2 hours, checking for tenderness at the 1½-hour mark. You want to achieve fall-off-the-bone consistency, and creamy gravy. Moisten with additional stock if needed.

Remove the roasting pan from the oven, and allow to sit for 15 minutes. The sauce will thicken. Serve with your favorite rice or mashed potatoes.

Meat Loaf *with* Mushroom Gravy

SERVES 4 TO 6

This is not your grandma's meat loaf. I keep the meat moist by fortifying it with a flavorful drizzle of gravy. The aromatic scent of the sage, pepper, and garlic will make your mouth water, and the mushroom gravy is so good, you're sure to have more than one helping.

MEAT LOAF

1½ pounds ground beef

1 large egg

1 onion, finely chopped

¾ cup whole milk

¾ cup bread crumbs

¼ cup ketchup

1 teaspoon kosher salt

½ teaspoon freshly ground black pepper

1 teaspoon garlic powder

1 teaspoon dried sage

MUSHROOM GRAVY

4 tablespoons (½ stick) unsalted butter

1 (16-ounce) package thinly-sliced cremini mushrooms

¾ teaspoon kosher salt

¼ teaspoon freshly ground black pepper

3 tablespoons all-purpose flour

1½ cups beef stock

1 teaspoon browning sauce (optional)

1 teaspoon chopped fresh parsley, for garnish

Preheat the oven to 350°F. Spray a glass 9-by-5-inch loaf pan with nonstick cooking spray.

Make the meat loaf: Combine the ground beef, egg, onion, milk, bread crumbs, ketchup, salt, pepper, garlic powder, and sage in a large bowl. Use your hands to mix fully.

Place the meat mixture in the prepared loaf pan and shape, filling to about 1 inch from the rim. Cover with foil, place on a baking sheet and bake for 1 hour to 1 hour and 15 minutes or until a meat thermometer registers 160°F.

Meanwhile, make the sauce: Heat the butter in a large sauté pan over medium-high heat for 1 minute. Add the mushrooms and cook for 4 to 5 minutes, until lightly browned. Season with the salt and pepper. Sprinkle the flour evenly over the top, stir to coat the mushrooms, and cook an additional minute. Add the beef stock and whisk constantly until smooth. Add the browning sauce, if using. Continue stirring and bring the sauce to a simmer until slightly thickened, about 1 to 2 minutes. Remove from the heat. Set aside.

Remove the loaf from the oven and allow to cool in the pan for 10 minutes. Drain any fat and liquid from the loaf pan after cooling for 10 minutes. Remove the loaf from the pan by placing a flat platter on top of the loaf pan and flipping it upside down. Slide the meat loaf out of the pan, using heat-resistant mitts. Slice and serve bathed in the delicious mushroom gravy, garnished with the parsley.

Meaty Beale Street Beans

SERVES 10

Where I'm from, people can be really particular about the beans brought to the cookout. "Who made these beans?" can be heard echoing throughout the party. Instead of boring baked beans out of the can, my recipe has a lot to offer with the use of ground beef, onions, and green peppers for flavor and texture. Once you get a taste of the sweet and tangy sauce made with mustard and barbecue sauce, your palate will jump with joy.

1 pound ground beef

1 white onion, chopped

1 green bell pepper, seeded and chopped

1 teaspoon garlic powder

1 teaspoon kosher salt

1 teaspoon freshly ground black pepper

2 (16-ounce) cans baked beans

2 tablespoons unsalted butter, melted

1 tablespoon BBQ sauce (see page 100)

1 tablespoon yellow mustard

½ cup light brown sugar

⅓ cup granulated sugar

Preheat the oven to 400°F.

Combine the beef, onion, and bell pepper in a large skillet over medium-high heat. Season with the garlic powder, salt, and black pepper. Cook for 6 minutes, or until the meat is completely browned and the veggies are tender. Set aside.

Pour the baked beans into a 2-quart casserole dish. Add the butter, BBQ sauce, mustard, brown sugar, sugar, and ground beef mixture. Stir well.

Bake, uncovered, for 35 minutes or until bubbling hot. Remove from the oven and allow to cool for 5 minutes before serving.

Slow Cooker Black-Eyed Peas

SERVES 8

This is simple country comfort food at its best. Savory, smoky, and spiced up with red pepper, my black-eyed peas are packed with flavor that will give you energy. Short on time? Put this in your slow cooker before you head out for the day and come home to a rich and creamy dinner that is not only healthy but also delicious. Serve over rice for a Quad-style Southern Hoppin' John.

8 cups chicken stock

1 pound dried black-eyed peas, soaked overnight and rinsed

2 large yellow onions, diced

2 green bell peppers, seeded and diced

2 red bell peppers, seeded and diced

2 celery ribs, diced

4 carrots, diced

1 smoked turkey leg

1 tablespoon ground cumin

1 teaspoon red pepper flakes

1 teaspoon cayenne pepper

1 teaspoon kosher salt

1 teaspoon freshly ground black pepper

Cooked rice, for serving

Pour the chicken stock into a slow cooker. Add the black-eyed peas, onions, bell peppers, celery, carrots, turkey leg, cumin, red pepper flakes, cayenne, salt, and pepper. Stir to combine.

Cover the slow cooker with its lid and set the heat to LOW. Cook for 8 hours, or until the black-eyed peas are tender.

Remove the turkey leg and pick all the meat from the bone. Stir the pulled turkey meat into the beans until combined.

Serve hot over rice.

GRILLIN' *and* CHILLIN': BBQ *with* MISS QUAD

When the summertime hits, no one can resist pulling out the grill for a good ole family cookout. From children playing tag to people indulging in a game of horseshoe, cooking on the grill brings family and friends together in love, unity, and community. It's a good shindig. But hold on now, don't let the villain called winter stop you. These days, smokeless grills make it easy to chill inside, and oven roasting works well, too.

Hawaiian Shrimp Kebabs *with* Sweet Chili Sauce

MAKES 10 SKEWERS

When visiting Hawaii, I formed an appreciation for the delicious taste combination of sweet and savory that instantly makes for a satisfied palate. These Hawaiian shrimp kebabs are a simple way to bring the island's finesse right to your kitchen. In my opinion, the chili sauce has just enough kick to make you want to hula dance.

SWEET CHILI SAUCE

3 garlic cloves, minced

2 teaspoons minced fresh ginger

1½ teaspoons red pepper flakes

1 tablespoon cornstarch

⅓ cup rice vinegar

1 tablespoon soy sauce

⅔ cup honey

¼ cup water

KEBABS

2 pounds jumbo shrimp, peeled and deveined

½ teaspoon kosher salt

1 teaspoon freshly ground black pepper

½ teaspoon paprika

1 pineapple, cut into 1-inch chunks

1 large red onion, cut into 1-inch chunks

1 large red bell pepper, seeded and cut into 1-inch chunks

1 large green bell pepper, seeded and cut into 1-inch chunks

Olive oil, for brushing

Prepare the sauce: Whisk together all the sauce ingredients in a saucepan over medium-low heat. Allow the sauce to thicken for 2 to 3 minutes, then remove from the heat and set aside.

Preheat a grill to medium-high heat.

Prepare the shrimp: Place the shrimp in a bowl and season with the salt, black pepper, and paprika. Alternately thread the shrimp and pineapple, onion, and bell peppers onto 10 skewers. Brush each side of the kebabs with the oil.

Place the shrimp on the grill. Cook until the shrimp become opaque on both sides and the pineapple and veggies begin to char, 2 to 3 minutes per side.

Transfer to a serving platter, drizzle with the sauce, and serve immediately.

Grilled Steak Kebabs

MAKES 12 KEBABS

There's nothing I like more than serving good food to friends, and these kebabs are the perfect centerpiece to any casual get-together. Make sure you give yourself enough time to marinate the steak, so the flavor really gets in there. You can grill these outside or inside—my smokeless indoor grill comes in very handy when I want to cook and chat by my kitchen island.

MARINADE

1 cup olive oil

2 tablespoons Worcestershire sauce

¼ cup smoky BBQ sauce

¼ cup soy sauce

1 tablespoon red wine vinegar

1 tablespoon fresh lemon juice

4 garlic cloves, minced

1 teaspoon freshly ground black pepper

KEBABS

2 pounds top sirloin steak, cut into
   1-inch pieces

Oil for grilling

1 red bell pepper

1 orange bell pepper

1 yellow bell pepper

1 medium red onion

Prepare the marinade: Combine all the marinade ingredients in a bowl. Setting aside about ½ cup of the marinade in the fridge to use for glazing the meat, add the steak pieces to the remaining marinade and toss to coat. Cover the bowl with plastic wrap and refrigerate overnight.

Thirty minutes before you're ready to grill, place 12 wooden skewers in water to soak.

Oil and preheat a grill to medium-high heat. Take the meat out of the refrigerator and set the bowl on the counter while you prepare the vegetables. (The meat will cook more evenly if it's not ice cold.) Halve and seed the peppers and cut into 1-inch pieces. Quarter the onion and separate into pieces.

Alternate placing the beef and vegetables on the skewers. Place the skewers on the grill. Turn the skewers every 2 to 3 minutes, using the reserved marinade to glaze the kebabs each time you turn them, until all sides are browned with some charring and the vegetables are tender, 10 to 12 minutes overall.

Allow the kebabs to rest for 5 minutes before serving.

Memphis Dry Rub Ribs

SERVES 4

I love me some ribs, any kind you want to serve up. Being that I'm from that beautiful city that sits on the bluff (Memphis, Tennessee, that is), I like my ribs dry-rubbed. We make them with a dry rub that imparts lots of flavors. My rub has some heat, as I'm sure you expect from me by now. It's so tasty that I make a big batch and keep it in several jars in my cupboard. (It's good on pork chops, lamb chops, any chops, and steaks too.) These baby back pork ribs have a pineapple glaze that makes them tender as can be. I could eat these ribs once a week!

DRY RUB

2 tablespoons paprika

1 tablespoon brown sugar

1 tablespoon kosher salt

1 teaspoon allspice

1 teaspoon cayenne pepper

2 teaspoons seasoning salt

2 teaspoons freshly ground black pepper

1 teaspoon garlic powder

2 teaspoons onion powder

½ teaspoon cumin

RIBS

1 cup pineapple juice

3 tablespoons cider vinegar

4 pounds baby back ribs

Preheat the grill to 300°F.

In a small bowl combine all the dry rub ingredients. Mix well.

Next, in small mixing bowl, whisk together the pineapple juice and cider vinegar to make the glaze. Set aside.

Place the ribs flat on a sheet pan or cutting board. Sprinkle liberally with the dry rub mixture and fully saturate both sides. Pat roughly to ensure entire rib is covered.

Place ribs with the meatier side down on the grill. Cover and cook for about an hour. After the first 20 minutes, brush both sides of ribs with the glaze. Repeat again at 40 minutes, and again just before removing the ribs from the grill.

Preheat the oven to 325°F. To finish cooking and impart more flavor to the ribs, place them into a roasting pan. Pour any remaining glaze over the ribs, and roast for 20 minutes uncovered, or until internal temp of 200°F.

Remove ribs from the oven and transfer to a cutting board. Allow the ribs to rest for 10 minutes and then cut ribs in between the bones.

Grilled Lamb Chops

SERVES 2

Lamb chops are an expensive cut of meat, so there is nothing more disappointing than over-marinating and making them too salty! That's why I created this recipe to ensure your lamb chops are just right and will leave your guests wanting more. I prefer to marinate my meat with the mix of garlic, rosemary sprigs, olive oil, salt, and black pepper, but to make it a little spicier, I add a few red pepper flakes. This marinade gives the lamb an unforgettable flavor! Pair it with my Shredded Cabbage Salad (page 85) and this is a meal you'll never forget.

¼ cup olive oil

2 garlic cloves, minced

1 teaspoon kosher salt

½ teaspoon freshly ground black pepper

½ teaspoon red pepper flakes

Fresh rosemary leaves from one sprig plus 6 whole rosemary sprigs

6 fresh lamb lollipop chops

Lawry's Steak & Chop Marinade

Preheat an indoor grill to medium-high heat or heat a grill pan over medium-high heat.

Combine the oil, garlic, salt, pepper, red pepper flakes, and rosemary leaves in a bowl to create a marinade for lamb chops.

Rinse the lamb lollipops under cold water, then pat dry. Spoon the marinade mixture completely over each lamb lollipop to coat on both sides.

Place the lamb on the grill or grill pan. Place one of the remaining rosemary sprigs atop each lamb lollipop. Grill for 3 to 4 minutes on each side, transferring the rosemary to the second side when you turn the lamb.

Before plating lightly brush with Lawry's Steak & Chop Marinade for enhanced flavor.

Transfer directly from the grill to a platter, and let rest for 5 to 10 minutes before serving.

Memphis BBQ Pulled Pork

SERVES 12

Great pulled pork? It's all about the dry rub and, let me tell you, I'm bringing it home with my spicy take! You'll have to give the meat a day to absorb all the great flavors, and then roast it with quartered onions. There's a sauce, too—I'm not holding out on you, friend. My sauce is nice and tart with a cider vinegar base and freshly ground pepper. You got some sweetness in there, too, with brown sugar and ketchup. A dash of liquid smoke pulls it together. You won't know what hit you!

DRY RUB

¼ cup sweet paprika

¼ cup brown sugar

3 tablespoons chili powder

3 tablespoons garlic powder

3 tablespoons kosher salt

2 tablespoons dry mustard

1 tablespoon cayenne

1 tablespoon freshly ground black
    pepper

PORK

4 to 5 pounds shoulder or butt pork roast

4 large yellow onions, quartered

BBQ SAUCE

2 cups cider vinegar

4 garlic cloves, minced

1 cup brown mustard

1 cup ketchup

½ cup brown sugar

1 teaspoon kosher salt

1 teaspoon freshly ground black pepper

1 teaspoon chili powder

1 teaspoon liquid smoke

Prepare the dry rub: Stir together all the rub ingredients in a bowl. Rub the mixture all over the pork shoulder. Cover the pork with plastic wrap and refrigerate overnight.

The following day, preheat the oven to 325°F.

Place the onion quarters on the bottom of a large roasting pan. Unwrap the pork shoulder and lay it on top of the onions. Roast for 6½ hours, or until fork-tender. Remove the pork and onions from the pan.

Prepare the BBQ sauce: Finely dice the roasted onions and add them back to the pan. Place the pan over medium-low heat. Add all the BBQ sauce ingredients and stir. Allow the sauce to simmer and reduce for about 10 minutes, or until thickened.

Meanwhile, using two forks, shred the pork shoulder meat apart.

Combine the pulled pork with the sauce, a cup at a time, until evenly coated. You will have sauce left over.

Sun-Dried Tomato Cornish Hen

SERVES 2

Are you hesitant about eating Cornish hen because you think it can taste a little gamey? Well, I am here to change your mind with this recipe! By adding special touches of honey and sun-dried tomatoes, the meat stays sweet and gives a fresh and savory taste that also complements the rosemary and thyme. This dish is perfect for eating solo.

2 Cornish hens

1 teaspoon kosher salt

1 teaspoon freshly ground black pepper

4 garlic cloves, sliced

2 rosemary sprigs

2 thyme sprigs

1 (8-ounce) jar oil-packed sun-dried
    tomatoes, chopped

1 tablespoon vegetable oil

1 teaspoon honey

½ teaspoon dried parsley

Preheat the oven to 425°F. Place a rack in a large roasting pan.

Clean the Cornish hen inside and out with running cold water, then pat dry.

Season the inside of the hen with ½ teaspoon each of the salt and pepper, the garlic, one of the rosemary sprigs, and the thyme sprigs. Place, breast side down, on the rack in the roasting pan.

Lightly lift up the skin of the hen around the breast and thigh. Nestle the sun-dried tomatoes and remaining rosemary between the skin and the flesh, then replace the skin and coat the entire hen with the oil, honey, additional salt and pepper, and the parsley.

Place the roasting pan on the center rack of the oven. Roast the hen for 30 minutes, then flip the hen and drizzle the excess drippings in the bottom of the pan over the hen. Roast for an additional 30 minutes.

Remove from the oven and allow to rest, then transfer to a serving dish.

Take your time, practice makes perfect.

"In order to get better and continue to build confidence, you must practice. My friend Niecy used to only cook when she was preparing a meal for a potential love interest. For the longest time, her sister cooked all of her meals, so when she did need to make her "catch-a-man meal," she became intimidated and overwhelmed with anxiety and she would have to call her sister. Eventually, she realized she was tired of needing someone to cook for, so she decided that she would learn to cook for herself and not have to depend on her sister. She eventually forced herself to get into the kitchen on a more regular basis. Although she is not yet an expert, her newly found confidence has made her more comfortable and happier in the kitchen.

Spicy Basil Grilled Chicken Breast

MAKES 4 BREASTS

This simple recipe can be grilled outdoors or in a grill pan. It's great for a family meal or a romantic dinner. The basil and cilantro marinade has just the right amount of flavor to wake you up, while the heat from the cayenne pepper will put your senses in overdrive. I like serving it over a bed of rice, paired with my Kale Citrus Salad (page 89).

¼ cup extra virgin olive oil

½ cup packed fresh basil

¼ cup packed fresh cilantro

Juice of 1 lime

1 teaspoon ground cayenne, or to taste

1 jalapeño pepper, halved, seeded, and diced

8 garlic cloves

4 boneless, skinless chicken breasts

In a food processor, process the olive oil, basil, cilantro, lime juice, cayenne, and jalapeño. Add the garlic and process just until finely chopped.

Coat chicken breasts with basil marinade. Cover in plastic wrap and set aside for at least 15 minutes or up to 2 hours.

Preheat grill to 325°F.

When the grill is ready, cook marinated chicken breasts for 5 minutes, then flip and cook for another 5 minutes. Remove from the grill.

Serve with your favorite side dishes.

Tip: You can use any fresh chili peppers you like. To make the marinade spicier, include some of the pepper's seeds.

Grilled Street Corn
with Truffle Oil Pico de Gallo

MAKES 6 EARS OF CORN

My take on street corn features a homemade pico de gallo, a lime-and-chili butter, and a liberal sprinkling of Cotija and cilantro. I don't shuck my corn completely because it feels festive to leave the husky skirts at the bottom. It makes the perfect handle for eating, too.

6 ears of corn

PICO DE GALLO

2 Roma tomatoes, diced

1 shallot, diced

Juice of 1 lime

3 tablespoons truffle oil

Salt and freshly ground black pepper, to taste

SPICY BUTTER

8 tablespoons (1 stick) unsalted butter, at room temperature

2 teaspoons chili powder

¼ teaspoon garlic powder

Juice of 1 lime

½ teaspoon kosher salt

¼ teaspoon freshly ground black pepper

FOR SERVING

½ cup Cotija

3 tablespoons chopped fresh cilantro

Peel back the leaves and remove the silks from the corn, without pulling off the leaves completely.

Prepare the pico de gallo: Combine all the pico de gallo ingredients in a bowl and set aside.

Heat a grill to medium-high.

While it is heating, prepare the spicy butter: Combine all the spicy butter ingredients in a bowl.

Spread the butter mixture evenly on the ears of corn and grill on all sides, until some spots begin to char, 4 to 6 minutes per side. Remove from the grill and set on a platter.

Sprinkle the corn with the Cotija, pico de gallo, and cilantro.

Note: You'll love this butter for more than corn. Use it on steak, garlic bread, or melted over roasted veggies.

DRINKS *on* ME! COCKTAILS *for Any* OCCASION

How about a drink? I don't have to tell you that libations are for almost any occasion, whether it is to relax after a long day of work, toasting to the weekend, or celebrating a special occasion. These recipes will have you toasting to the good life!

Peach Vodka Cocktail

MAKES 1 COCKTAIL

If you're looking for a sweet and citrusy cocktail to help lift your spirits, this is the drink! Best served chilled and neat, although it's fine over ice in a high ball glass, I find that it pairs well with protein such as my Beef Short Ribs (page 173) or my Grilled Steak Kebabs (page 191) and it won't weigh down the meal.

⅓ cup ice

½ ounce peach schnapps

½ ounce freshly squeezed lemon juice

1½ ounces vodka

1 ounce seltzer

Fresh peach slices, for garnish

Combine the ice with the peach schnapps, lemon juice, and vodka in a cocktail shaker and shake well for 7 to 10 seconds.

Strain the chilled drink into a margarita glass. Top with seltzer and garnish with the peach slices.

Quad's Bloody Mary

MAKES 1 COCKTAIL

This is nothing like your grandma's Bloody Mary! This morning brunch drink can be served with or without alcohol, and will wake you up with its peppery and rich flavor. Personally, I think this is best served with my Potato, Ham, and Cheese Frittata (page 26).

1 teaspoon kosher salt

1 teaspoon paprika

Pinch of cayenne pepper

2 ounces vodka

1 ounce rum

5 ounces Bloody Mary mix

Dash of hot sauce

1 celery stalk

Pepperoncini

Olives

Pickle spear (optional)

Stir together the salt, paprika, and cayenne in a small bowl.

Fill a cocktail shaker with ice, then pour in the vodka, Bloody Mary mix, half of the spice mixture, and the hot sauce. Shake well for 10 to 12 seconds.

Pour into a pilsner glass and top with the remaining spice mixture. Garnish with the celery stalk, pepperoncini, olives, and pickle spear, if using.

White Wine Sangria

SERVES 6

Who doesn't love a great sangria? The added fruit makes it very enticing! It looks so amazing that I wanted to feature it on the cover of my book. While sangria is mostly served in the summer, don't be afraid to try it with brunch anytime of the year.

4 cups ice

1 bottle white wine, such as pinot or sauvignon blanc

⅓ cup fresh orange juice

¾ cup pineapple juice

1 red apple, thinly sliced

1 green apple, thinly sliced

1 orange, thinly sliced

⅓ cup hulled and sliced strawberries

⅓ cup blackberries

Place 4 cups of ice in a large pitcher, then add the wine, orange juice, pineapple juice, apples, oranges, strawberries, and blackberries and stir well.

Chill the pitcher in the fridge for 30 minutes before serving the sangria in chilled glasses.

Note: You can really go to town with the fruit here. I like adding kiwi, blueberries, raspberries—whatever is fresh and available. Sometimes I top it off with bubbles too, in the form of prosecco!

Glenlivet Mule

You'll love this Scottish twist on the Moscow Mule. The tasty and earthy flavor of the scotch combines with Grand Marnier for a savory citrus taste that lingers on the tongue. Garnish it with mint and you'll be off to the races!

1½ ounces Glenlivet Reserve Scotch

1 ounce Grand Marnier

1 ounce ginger beer

3 ounces Prosecco

Mint sprig, for garnish

Lime wheel, for garnish

Combine the scotch, Grand Marnier, ginger beer, and ice in a copper mule mug and stir.

Top with the Prosecco and garnish with the mint sprig and lime wheel. Served chilled.

Prosecco Spritzer

MAKES 1 COCKTAIL

Even though this is one of my favorite summer cocktails, this spritzer can easily be enjoyed any time of the year. Poured in a champagne flute with a splash of the deliciously floral St. Germain, this drink is refreshing and light. Serve it chilled with a twist of lemon and it's instantly the perfect drink for lunch or brunch. Sometimes I add fresh pomegranate seeds for a festive garnish.

½ ounce St. Germain

4 ounces Prosecco

Lemon twist and fresh pomegranate seeds, for garnish, if desired

In a champagne flute, add the St. Germain. Top with Prosecco. Twist lemon peel and add to glass along with pomegranate seeds, if using.

Cabernet Sangria

SERVES 6

I love a good wine with dinner, but sometimes you're looking for a little more. Bring on the fruit! You will love the taste of this cabernet sangria that is not only refreshing but also complements my spicy dishes. It's great with shrimp, creating the perfect infusion of sweet and succulent.

4 cups ice

3 oranges, sliced thinly

1 lemon, sliced thinly

1 lime, sliced thinly

1 bottle cabernet sauvignon

½ cup brandy

⅓ cup triple sec

Place 4 cups of ice, and the orange, lemon, and lime slices in a large pitcher.

Add the cabernet sauvignon, brandy, and triple sec and stir.

Chill the pitcher in the fridge for 30 minutes before serving. Serve in large tumblers.

Blueberry Bourbon Lemonade

MAKES 1 COCKTAIL

A great summer drink, this spiked lemonade looks sweet but it can sneak up on you! The sweet and smoky flavor of the bourbon is a perfect pairing with my Spicy Sage Sausage Flatbread Topped with Fried Eggs (page 25) or my Savory Cornmeal Pancakes (page 32), creating a brunch to remember. Thank me later!

6 blueberries, plus more for serving

1½ ounces bourbon

½ ounce simple syrup

3 ounces lemonade

⅓ ounce fresh lemon juice

Lemon wheel, for garnish

⅓ ounce seltzer (optional)

Crush the blueberries in a cocktail shaker until the bottom of the shaker is filled with juice. Fill with ice.

Pour in the bourbon, simple syrup, lemonade, and lemon juice. Shake well for 5 to 7 seconds.

Pour into an old-fashioned or highball glass. Garnish with additional blueberries and the lemon wheel. For a refreshing sip, top with splash of seltzer.

Acknowledgments

Thanks to my partners at The Countryman Press who helped to make my dream possible: Ron Lange, Michael Levatino, Steven Pace, LeAnna Weller Smith, Nicholas Teodoro, Ann Treistman, Tracy Vega, Jess Murphy, and Devon Zahn.

I am deeply grateful for the countless phone calls filled with words of encouragement, insight, and guidance.

Thanks, Pat Neeley, for celebrating me.

Special thanks to my team:

Marilyn Allen

Danika Berry

Will Sterling

Cam Dangerfield

Raz

Thom Driver

Tweety E

And most importantly, thanks to my loving mom. I love you!

Photo Credits

Pages 22–23: © Sokorevaphoto/iStockPhoto.com; page 29: © A Sundberg Photography/Shutterstock.com; page 30: © Julia_Sudnitskaya/iStockPhoto.com; pages 46, 90–91, 98, 105, 143, 162, 176, 232: © bhofack2/iStockPhoto.com; pages 49, 66: © rudisill/iStockPhoto.com; page 65: © czardases/iStockPhoto.com; page 84: © Olha_Afanasieva/iStockPhoto.com; page 94: © Brent Hofacker/iStockPhoto.com; pages 106–107: © yulkapopkova/iStockPhoto.com; page 108: © haoliang/iStockPhoto.com; page 119: © eskymaks/iStockPhoto.com; page 122: © Ravsky/iStockPhoto.com; page 124: © Nikolay_Donetsk/iStockPhoto.com; pages 126–127, 195: © LauriPatterson/iStockPhoto.com; page 131: © imagesbybarbara/iStockPhoto.com; page 132: © Anna_Shepulova/iStockPhoto.com; page 135: © Sergiy Artsaba/Shutterstock.com; page 140: © iuliia_n/Shutterstock.com; pages 166–167: © Aimee M Lee/Shutterstock.com; page 171: © Bill Oxford/iStockPhoto.com; pages 172, 182: © casanisa/Shutterstock.com; page 175: © Ken Cave/iStockPhoto.com; page 179: © graytown/iStockPhoto.com; page 185: © Annmarie Young/Shutterstock.com; page 214: © AnnaPustynnikova/iStockPhoto.com; page 217: © ddsign_stock/iStockPhoto.com; page 218: © AnaMOMarques/iStockPhoto.com

Index

Note: Page numbers in *italic* refer to photographs.